ARCTIC TUNDRA
and POLAR DESERTS

Chris Woodford

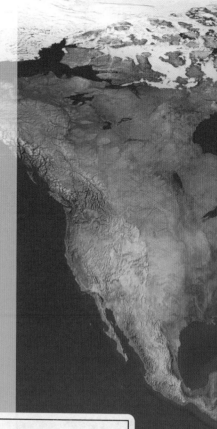

www.raintreepublishers.co.uk
Visit our website to find out more information about Raintree books.

To order:
☎ Phone 0845 6044371
🖨 Fax +44 (0) 1865 312263
✉ Email myorders@raintreepublishers.co.uk

Customers from outside the UK please telephone +44 1865 312262

Raintree is an imprint of Capstone Global Library Limited, a company incorporated in England and Wales having its registered office at 7 Pilgrim Street, London, EC4V 6LB – Registered company number: 6695582

Text © Capstone Global Library Limited 2011
First published in hardback in 2011
The moral rights of the proprietor have been asserted.

For The Brown Reference Group
Editorial Director: Lindsey Lowe
Managing Editor: Tim Harris
Editor: Jolyon Goddard
Original consultant: Dr. Mark Hostetler, Department of Wildlife Ecology and Conservation, University of Florida
Designers: Reg Cox, Joan Curtis
Picture Researcher: Clare Newman
Production Director: Alastair Gourlay
Printed in the USA

ISBN: 978 1 406 21791 9

14 13 12 11 10
10 9 8 7 6 5 4 3 2 1

British Library Cataloguing in Publication Data
Woodford, Chris.
  Arctic tundra and polar deserts. -- (Biomes atlases)
  1. Tundra ecology--Juvenile literature. 2. Ecology--Polar regions--Juvenile literature. I. Title II. Series
  577.5'86-dc22
A full catalogue record for this book is available from the British Library.

The acknowledgments on p. 64 form part of this copyright page. Every effort has been made to contact copyright holders of material reproduced in this book. Any omissions will be rectified in subsequent printings if notice is given to the publisher.

Disclaimer
All the Internet addresses (URLs) given in this book were valid at the time of going to press. However, due to the dynamic nature of the Internet, some addresses may have changed, or sites may have changed or ceased to exist since publication. While the author and publisher regret any inconvenience this may cause readers, no responsibility for any such changes can be accepted by either the author or the publisher.

About this Book

The introductory pages of this book describe the biomes of the world and then the polar biomes. The five main chapters look at different aspects of the polar biomes: climate, plants, animals, people and the future. Between the chapters are detailed maps that focus on key places within the biomes. The map pages are shown in the contents in italics, *like this*. Exclamation-mark icons on the map pages draw attention to regions where the biome or its wildlife is under threat. Throughout the book you'll also find boxed stories or fact files about the polar biomes. The icons here show what the boxes are about. Words in **bold** throughout the book are explained in the glossary at the end of the book. After the glossary is a list of books and websites for further research and an index, allowing you to find subjects anywhere in the book.

 Climate

 People

 Plants

 Future

 Animals

 Facts

 Extinction

 Under Threat

Contents

Biomes of the World   4

The Polar Biomes   6

North American Arctic   8

Polar Climate   10

Siberian Tundra   18

Polar Plants   20

Iceland   26

Polar Animals   28

Antarctica   42

People and the Poles   44

Greenland   54

The Future   56

Glossary   62

Further Research   63

Index   64

BIOMES OF THE WORLD

Biologists divide the living world into major zones named biomes. Each biome has its own distinctive climate, plants and animals.

If you were to walk all the way from the north of Canada to the Amazon **rainforest**, you'd notice the wilderness changing dramatically along the way.

Northern Canada is a freezing and barren place without trees, where only tiny brownish-green plants can survive in the icy ground. But trudge south for long enough and you enter a magical world of conifer forests, where moose, caribou and wolves live. After several weeks, the conifers give out, and you reach the grass-covered prairies of the central United States. The further south you go, the drier the land gets and the hotter the Sun feels, until you find yourself hiking through a cactus-filled **desert**. But once you reach southern Mexico, the cacti start to disappear, and strange, **tropical** trees begin to take their place. Here, the muggy air is filled with the calls of exotic birds and the drone of tropical insects. Finally, in Colombia you cross the Andes mountain range – whose chilly peaks remind you a little of your starting point – and descend into the dense, swampy jungles of the Amazon rainforest.

Desert is the driest biome. There are hot deserts and cold ones.

Taiga is made up of conifer trees that can survive freezing winters.

Scientists have a special name for the different regions – such as desert, tropical rainforest and prairie – that you'd pass through on such a journey. They call them **biomes**. Everywhere on Earth can be classified as being in one biome or another, and the same biome often appears in lots of

4

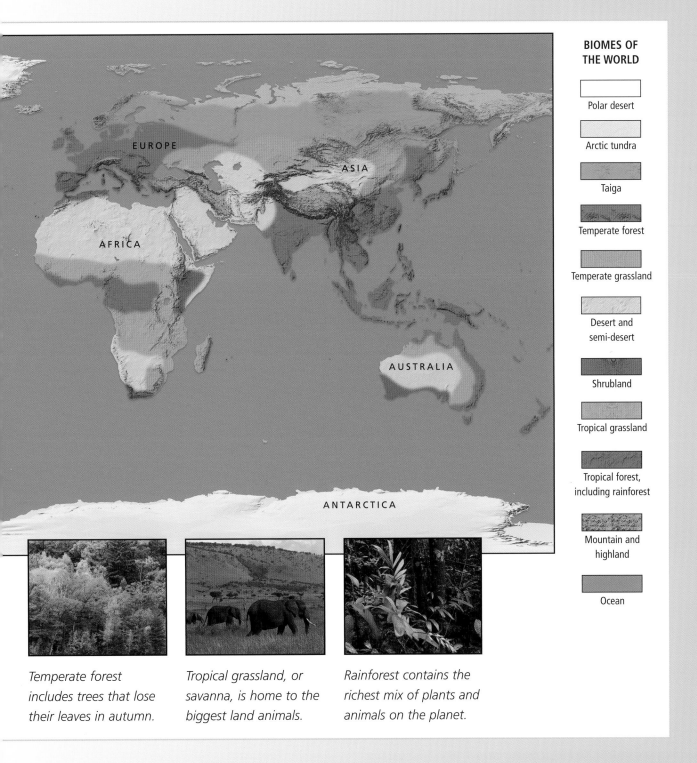

BIOMES OF
THE WORLD

Polar desert

Arctic tundra

Taiga

Temperate forest

Temperate grassland

Desert and
semi-desert

Shrubland

Tropical grassland

Tropical forest,
including rainforest

Mountain and
highland

Ocean

EUROPE

ASIA

AFRICA

AUSTRALIA

ANTARCTICA

*Temperate forest
includes trees that lose
their leaves in autumn.*

*Tropical grassland, or
savanna, is home to the
biggest land animals.*

*Rainforest contains the
richest mix of plants and
animals on the planet.*

different places. For instance, there are areas
of rainforest as far apart as Brazil, Africa and
Southeast Asia. Although the plants
and animals that inhabit these forests are
different, they live in similar ways. Likewise,
the prairies of North America are part of the
grassland biome, which also occurs in China,

Australia and Argentina. Wherever there are
grasslands, there are grazing animals that feed
on the grass, as well as large carnivores that
hunt and kill the grazers.

The map on this page shows how the
world's major biomes fit together to make
up the biosphere – the zone of life on Earth.

5

THE POLAR BIOMES

Next time you open your freezer, think what it would be like to live in an icy cold place. Perhaps you would need a layer of blubbery fat to keep you warm. Or maybe you would have a thick hairy coat and stand still for long periods.

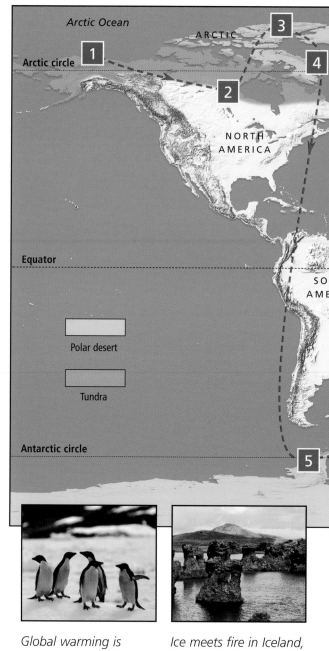

Polar desert

Tundra

Global warming is causing a reduction of ice in Antarctica.

Ice meets fire in Iceland, where volcanoes and hot springs warm the tundra.

Biting cold is only one of the problems of living near the poles. But it is the main reason that the Arctic (the region near the North Pole) and the Antarctic (the region near the South Pole) are such challenging places for animals and plants to survive in. The weather is coldest close to the poles, but milder further away. Scientists therefore divide the polar regions into two different biomes: arctic **tundra** and **polar desert**.

Because the ground is frozen in the far north, trees cannot grow. Between the point where trees stop growing and the coast of the Arctic Ocean lies the tundra. It takes up about a tenth of Earth's surface and covers the most northern parts of North America, Europe and Asia. Wild, barren and frozen solid in winter, the tundra bursts into life during summer in a swampy patchwork of colourful plants. Animals as different as the

musk ox and the arctic hare make this their home. Although there are many lakes and ponds formed from melting ice, much of the tundra gets as little rain as a desert.

Both the northern Arctic and the whole of Antarctica are too cold even for the hardy plants and animals of the tundra. The land

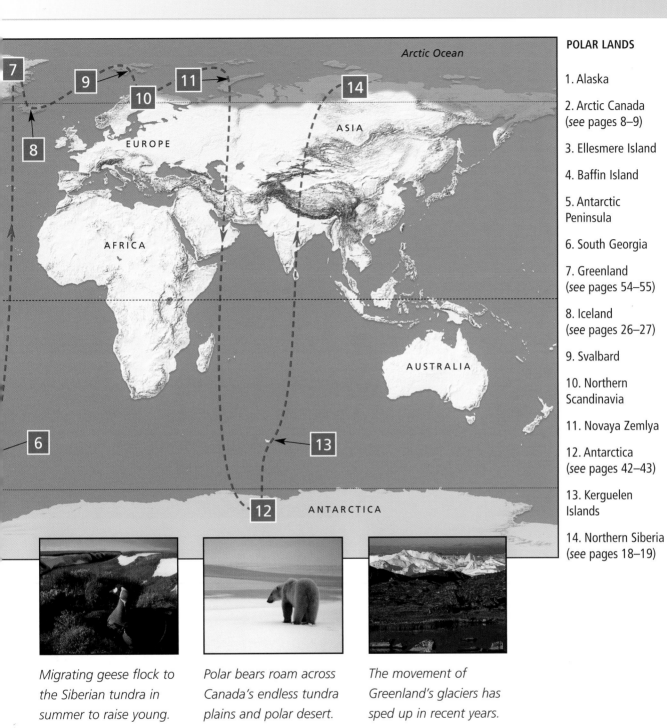

7

9

10

11

14

8

EUROPE

ASIA

AFRICA

AUSTRALIA

6

13

12

ANTARCTICA

POLAR LANDS

1. Alaska

2. Arctic Canada
(*see pages 8–9*)

3. Ellesmere Island

4. Baffin Island

5. Antarctic
Peninsula

6. South Georgia

7. Greenland
(*see pages 54–55*)

8. Iceland
(*see pages 26–27*)

9. Svalbard

10. Northern
Scandinavia

11. Novaya Zemlya

12. Antarctica
(*see pages 42–43*)

13. Kerguelen
Islands

14. Northern Siberia
(*see pages 18–19*)

Migrating geese flock to the Siberian tundra in summer to raise young.

Polar bears roam across Canada's endless tundra plains and polar desert.

The movement of Greenland's glaciers has sped up in recent years.

there is either barren or covered with a permanent layer of ice that never thaws. There is even less rain or snow than in the tundra. As a result, this biome is known as polar desert. Very few plants and animals can survive year round in the polar desert. Seabirds nest there, but none are tough enough to survive entirely on land because there is not enough food. Most life in the polar desert is limited to the coast, where the animals can take food from the ocean. In recent years, scientists have voiced concern over the reduction of ice at both poles, which they have linked to **global warming**.

NORTH AMERICAN ARCTIC

The tundra and polar deserts of Canada and Alaska are the emptiest parts of North America. The animals and people who live here have to endure long, dark freezing winters, when temperatures can plunge to –50°C (–58°F).

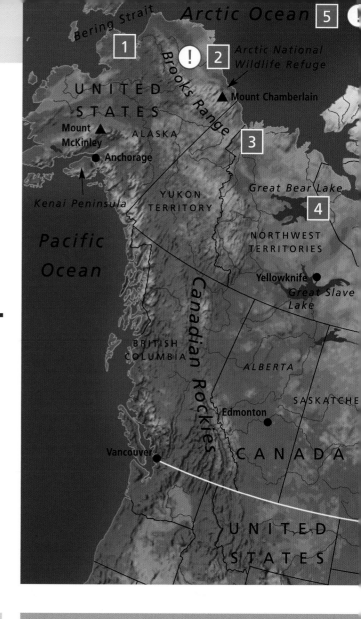

Bering Strait

Arctic Ocean 5

1

! 2 Arctic National Wildlife Refuge

▲ Mount Chamberlain

UNITED STATES

ALASKA

3

Mount ▲ McKinley

● Anchorage

Great Bear Lake

4

YUKON TERRITORY

NORTHWEST TERRITORIES

Kenai Peninsula

Pacific Ocean

Yellowknife ●

Great Slave Lake

Canadian Rockies

BRITISH COLUMBIA

ALBERTA

SASKATCHE

● Edmonton

Vancouver ●

CANADA

UNITED STATES

Fact File

▲ About 12,000 years ago, Canada was covered with ice and much of the United States was tundra. Tundra animals included mammoths, saber-toothed cats, lions, camels and bison.

▲ The tundra is still home to some remarkable creatures, including musk oxen, lemmings, polar bears and caribou. Global warming threatens the delicate balance of nature on the tundra.

▲ The United States bought Alaska from Russia in 1867 for just $7.2 million – roughly 5 cents a hectare (2 cents an acre). Its vast oil and mineral deposits now make it worth many times as much.

Dall sheep live in the rugged mountains of Alaska, where Inupiat people hunt them by snowmobile.

GREENLAND

+ North
magnetic pole

Ellesmere Island

Devon Island

Baffin Island

NAVUT

Iqaluit

Great Plain of
the Koukdjuak

Hudson Bay

ANITOBA

Hudson Bay Lowlands

Lake Winnipeg

ONTARIO

Winnipeg

Lake Superior

Atlantic Ocean

NEWFOUNDLAND

QUEBEC

St John's

PRINCE EDWARD ISLAND

NEW BRUNSWICK

Quebec

NOVA SCOTIA

Montreal

N

NORTH AMERICA

EUROPE

ASIA

AFRICA

SOUTH AMERICA

AUSTRALIA

ANTARCTICA

miles km
500
500
0 0

1. Bering Strait
A narrow gap between Alaska and Siberia, about 64 kilometres (40 miles) across.

2. Arctic National Wildlife Refuge
A protected area of Alaskan tundra that contains important breeding grounds for polar bears and caribou. The possibility of drilling for oil here was a major topic in the 2008 U.S. presidential race.

3. Brooks Range
A mountain range in Alaska. The highest point, Mount Chamberlain, is about a third the height of Mount Everest.

4. Great Bear Lake
A large freshwater lake – the largest entirely within Canada.

5. Arctic Ocean
The world's smallest ocean. During winter, most of the Arctic is covered with sea ice. Global warming is reducing the amount of ice, which could lead to a raise in sea levels.

6. North Magnetic Pole
The place to which compasses point. The magnetic pole is about 1,600 kilometres (1,000 miles) from the North Pole. It changes location slowly over the years.

7. Hudson Bay Lowlands
A vast area of swampy tundra and wetlands.

8. Ellesmere Island
Cape Columbia, at the top of the island, is the most northern part of North America. Its ice shelf is breaking up as a result of global warming.

9. Devon Island
Parts of this rocky desert island look just like Mars. NASA uses the island to test Martian probes and buggies.

10. Great Plain of the Koukdjuak
A wetland area with many rivers, ponds and streams.

Across the Bering Bridge

Between Alaska and Siberia is a narrow passage of water called the Bering Strait, but this has not always been there. During Earth's ice ages, the sea level fell as water turned to ice. As a result, the land between Alaska and Siberia emerged above sea level, forming a land bridge.

The land bridge across the Bering Strait allowed animals to walk across. Ancient species of horses and camels wandered west from Alaska to Asia and evolved into the zebras and camels we know today. Some animals moved east, including caribou (below), lemmings, foxes and wolves. The Native Americans, who were the first people to settle in North America, also probably crossed the Bering bridge.

9

POLAR CLIMATE

The pattern of weather that occurs in one region during a typical year is called the region's climate. In the Arctic and the Antarctic, the climate is very cold and dry, and this is why the polar biomes exist.

Have you ever stopped to wonder why there is snow and ice around the polar regions at the top and bottom of our planet, but not around the middle, where there are savannahs (**tropical grasslands**) and **tropical forests** instead? The answer lies in the way Earth moves as it travels through space.

Earth travels around the Sun in a giant circle called an orbit, taking a year to complete one orbit. Besides orbiting the Sun, our planet is continually spinning around, making one whole turn each day. Earth stays roughly upright as it spins, with the poles at the top and bottom. Because the poles never face the Sun directly, the sunlight they receive is spread over a wide area, and this is the reason why the poles are so cold compared to other parts of the planet. You'd notice the weak sunlight if you stood on the North Pole in the middle of a sunny day. Even in mid-summer the Sun would be very low in the sky, and its rays would hardly warm your skin.

Right: this photo shows the Sun in several different positions during its path across the sky on a mid-summer night in Antarctica. The middle two images of the Sun were produced around midnight. On this night, for viewers on the antarctic circle, the Sun does not set at all, but dips towards the horizon. The Sun then continues its wide circle around the sky.

The temperature in Antarctica rarely rises above freezing, even in mid-summer. There is hardly any liquid freshwater for plants to absorb.

The Midnight Sun

A strange thing about the polar regions is their unusual pattern of daylight. There is only one day and one night each year at the North and South Poles, each lasting six months. The Sun stays just above the horizon for six months of the year, circling through the sky once every 24 hours. It gradually sinks lower, until it disappears altogether for the next six months. Once the Sun has set, the pole is plunged into darkness for half a year, and the weather turns bitterly cold.

At the North Pole, the permanently dark winter lasts from 21 September to 21 March, with mid-winter on 21 December. The opposite happens at the South Pole, where it is summer from September to March.

The strange days and seasons happen because the poles lie at the ends of Earth's axis – the imaginary line around which our planet spins. While the rest of the planet spins around, turning through day and night every 24 hours, the poles stay in the same place, a bit like the ends of a spinning top. Because Earth's axis is slightly tilted, the poles take turns facing the Sun or facing away, and this is why they spend six months in sunlight followed by six months in darkness.

Arctic Circle

As you travel from the North Pole, the pattern of light and darkness becomes more normal. Once you reach the **arctic circle** – an imaginary circle drawn a certain distance around the North Pole – there is only one day each year when the Sun does not rise at all, and only one day when it does not set. The same happens at the **antarctic circle**.

Six months of continuous daylight might seem like enough to make the poles positively tropical places, but there are some complications. Not only is the Sun low in the sky, but the ice and snow at the poles reflect away most of the sunlight. As a result, most of the Sun's heat bounces straight back into space, and this makes the poles even more chilly than they would otherwise be.

Poles Apart

Many people think the Arctic and Antarctic are much the same, except for being on opposite ends of the world. But there are important differences. For one thing, the

Dark blue indicates high rainfall in these four world maps. The polar regions, like desert regions elsewhere, are very pale blue in both the January and July maps because they receive so little rain throughout the year. Red or orange areas of these maps are hot regions with high temperatures. Blue indicates low temperatures. The antarctic region is cold in both July and January, but the Arctic warms to higher temperatures in July.

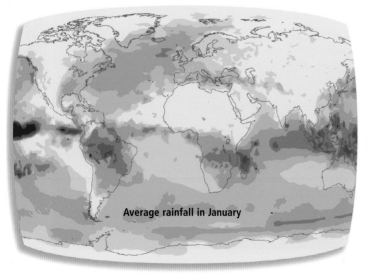

Average rainfall in January

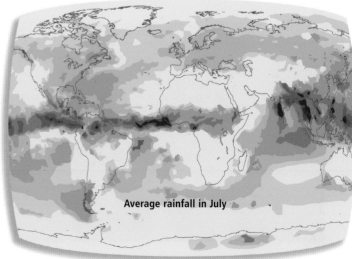

Average rainfall in July

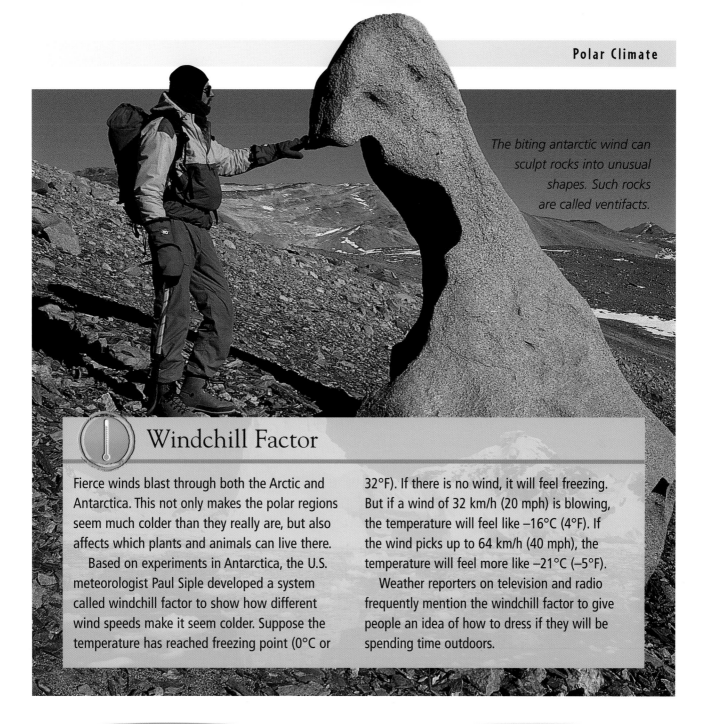

The biting antarctic wind can sculpt rocks into unusual shapes. Such rocks are called ventifacts.

Windchill Factor

Fierce winds blast through both the Arctic and Antarctica. This not only makes the polar regions seem much colder than they really are, but also affects which plants and animals can live there.

Based on experiments in Antarctica, the U.S. meteorologist Paul Siple developed a system called windchill factor to show how different wind speeds make it seem colder. Suppose the temperature has reached freezing point (0°C or 32°F). If there is no wind, it will feel freezing. But if a wind of 32 km/h (20 mph) is blowing, the temperature will feel like –16°C (4°F). If the wind picks up to 64 km/h (40 mph), the temperature will feel more like –21°C (–5°F).

Weather reporters on television and radio frequently mention the windchill factor to give people an idea of how to dress if they will be spending time outdoors.

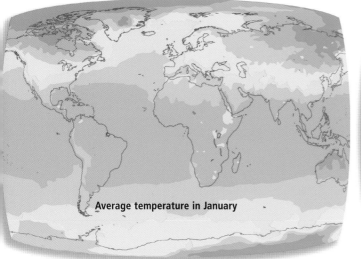

Average temperature in January

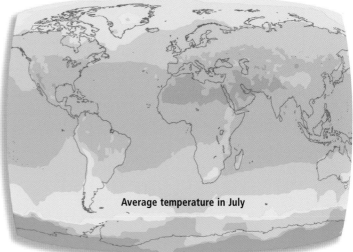

Average temperature in July

Arctic is mostly ocean below its layer of snow and ice, while a huge continent makes up most of the Antarctic. Although the surface of the Arctic Ocean is frozen, the water below keeps moving. A warm ocean current from the Atlantic keeps the Arctic warmer in winter than it would otherwise be. The surface ice moves and often splits, producing large stretches of open water. Nearby landmasses, such as Alaska and Siberia, also provide some heat. Antarctica, however, is cut off from warm waters by a cold ocean current that flows around the continent. It is also very far from other landmasses, and its surface is much higher than sea level, which makes it even colder.

Average winter temperatures in the Arctic vary greatly across the region, but typically reach lows of about –34°C (–30°F). The average temperature in the arctic summer is about 10°C (50°F). That is warm enough to thaw the frozen surface in the tundra region, allowing it to burst into life in the brief arctic summer.

Climographs

Each place in the world has its own pattern of weather. The typical pattern of weather that happens in one place during a year is called climate. It is possible to show a place's climate on a climograph, such as the one shown here for St. Louis. The letters along the bottom are the months of the year. The numbers on the left and the small bars show rainfall, and the numbers on the right and the curved line show temperature. You can see at a glance that St. Louis is hottest in July, but December is the driest month.

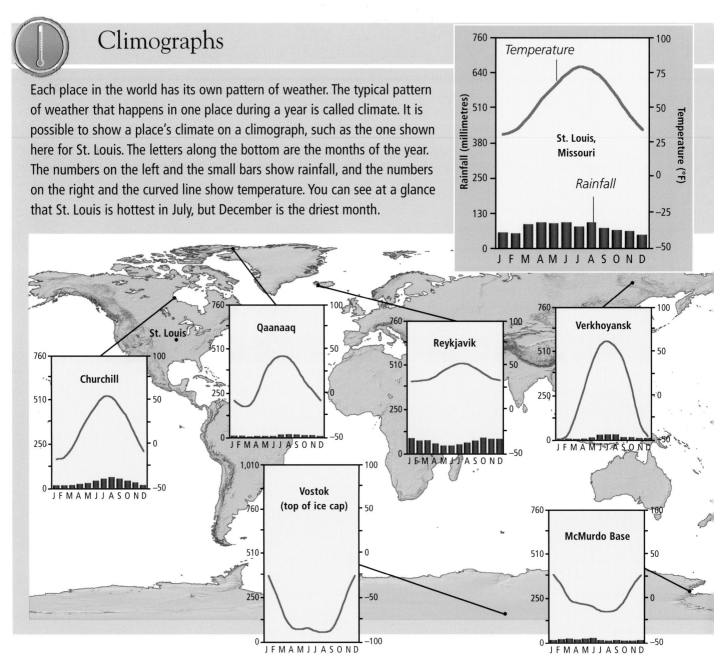

Antarctica is so dry that some parts, including the Dry Valleys, are free of ice. Visitors remark how the Dry Valleys seem like the surface of Mars. When NASA was testing vehicles for durability for its Viking mission to Mars in the 1970s, it brought them to the Dry Valleys.

The Arid Poles

The arid polar climate is caused by cold air sinking over the poles. The air in Earth's atmosphere is continually moving, rising in certain places and sinking in others. When air rises it cools down, and this makes moisture in the air turn to rain or snow, which fall back to Earth. Sinking air comes from high in the atmosphere, so it has already lost its moisture and become dry. As it hits the ground, it spreads outwards and stops moister air from moving in. The world's largest deserts and the poles lie in areas where dry air is continually sinking, resulting in clear blue skies and very dry weather.

The Arctic is warmer than most people believe. In the early 1990s, a Russian icebreaker forced its way through sea ice to the North Pole with a party of tourists on board. They held a barbecue at the pole, and some of them even went for a chilly swim! Swimming in the Antarctic Ocean is another matter. There, the average winter temperature is –26°C (–15°F), and the average summer temperature is only –3°C (26°F). High on top of the antarctic ice cap, the conditions are even more extreme: summer temperatures of –32°C (–26°F) drop to an average of –60°C (–76°F) in winter. In other words, summer on the antarctic **ice cap** is often colder even than an arctic winter. It is no place for a summer barbecue. If you made a hole in the antarctic ice and hauled out a small fish, it would freeze solid in minutes.

Water, Water, Everywhere?

Although there are masses of ice and snow at the poles, the Arctic and Antarctica are among the driest places on Earth. The South Pole receives only a small amount of snow (about 50 millimetres or 2 inches) each year.

Some parts of Antarctica receive less than a tenth of the rainfall or snow of a typical desert. The Dry Valleys of the Transantarctic Mountains are drier than the Sahara.

The Arctic is wetter than Antarctica, though it is still very dry. It typically gets about 200 millimetres (8 inches) of rain and snow each year, and the tundra tends to retain the water that falls there. There are two reasons for this: underneath the tundra is a layer of permanently frozen soil called **permafrost** through which water cannot seep away; and above the tundra is a layer of cold air. Cold air makes it difficult for water on the ground to **evaporate** (turn to vapour), because air can hold very little moisture when it is cold. Together, the permafrost and the cold air keep water sandwiched inside the tundra. In summer, the water trickles across the flat tundra landscape in small streams and rivers, or it collects in ponds, lakes and marshes.

15

Alpine Cold

The same cold conditions that create tundra landscapes in the Arctic also happen on high mountains elsewhere on Earth. A lot of plants that grow in the Arctic also grow on mountains. Tundra stretches into the Rockies far to the south of the Arctic. The conditions are not the same, though. Outside the Arctic, it is often far wetter, and the strange sequence of very dark winters and bright summers does not exist. The biome on top of high mountains is called alpine tundra, which is covered in more detail in the *Mountains* book of this series.

The Polar Seasons

If you visited the arctic tundra in summer and winter, you might think you had gone to two completely different places. In summer, when daylight lasts nearly 24 hours, the tundra is a mixture of green, treeless plains, swamps, bogs and lakes. In some places there is more water

Permafrost

If you dig a hole in your garden, you'll probably find nothing but damp brown soil. Try to do the same thing in the tundra, however, and your spade will suddenly scrape against a thick layer of permanently frozen soil: permafrost. Permafrost is so-called because it is permanently frosty, even in the middle of summer. It is usually about 50 centimetres (20 inches) below the tundra's surface, though in winter the top layer of soil is frozen, too.

Permafrost plays an important part in the tundra's ecology. It stops water from draining away, and so keeps the tundra wet and marshy in summer, like the tundra on Banks Island, Canada (below). Scientists are worried that global warming – the gradual warming of Earth's climate as a result of pollutants in the atmosphere – is now melting the permafrost in Siberia and other parts of the Arctic. This will harm the tundra and release methane into the atmosphere – a gas that, in turn, will increase global warming and climate change.

than land, and travelling can be difficult. For about two months in summer, the tundra comes alive with wildlife: insects such as mosquitoes and flies, wetland birds and fish, roaming grizzly bears, and swooping owls and jaegers are to be found. In winter, the Arctic is another world entirely. The tundra freezes solid, and ice covers the lakes, rivers and sea. Plants vanish beneath the blanket of ice, and most of the animals head south for winter. The nights grow so long that they seem to merge together, and blinding snowstorms can make it almost impossible to see.

In recent years, global warming has increased the length of the summer thaw in the Arctic. In Antarctica, much of the sea ice around the continent melts, but the land stays frozen. Only the coast can support seabirds and other animals briefly in summer. Most of these soon move away from Antarctica before winter. If global warming continues unchecked, Antarctica's land will thaw in summer, too.

Aurorae (the northern and southern lights) dance around the sky in the polar regions. They are caused by particles from the Sun hitting Earth's atmosphere.

SIBERIAN TUNDRA

A vast belt of tundra stretches across north Siberia in Russia, from the northern edge of the taiga to the coast of the Arctic Ocean. The Siberian tundra comes to life each year after the spring thaw. Countless ponds and lakes form from meltwater, and the ground turns into a carpet of mosses, lichens and flowering shrubs.

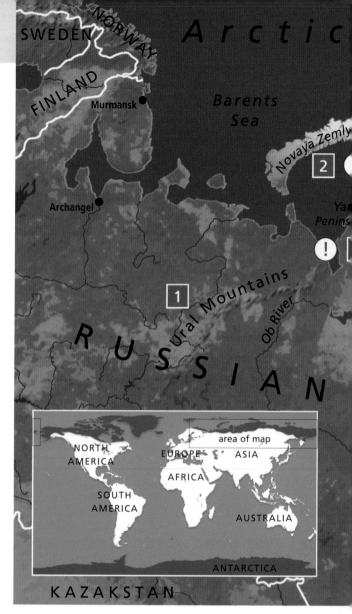

Tundra in Trouble

One of the biggest threats to Siberia's tundra comes from oil and gas extraction. In the past, wells took up vast areas. Vehicles and machinery crushed the fragile tundra plants, and caused the permafrost (frozen soil) to thaw earlier and collapse. It takes decades for the thin layer of soil to form again. People can now use modern techniques that are less destructive, but the tundra habitat may still suffer in less obvious ways.

Scientists are already seeing that melting permafrost has increased the flow of rivers into the Arctic Ocean. The extra water makes the ocean less salty and is damaging the habitats of many species. The melting may eventually cause the low-lying arctic tundra to sink into the sea.

1. Ural Mountains
This long mountain range separates Europe from Asia.

2. Novaya Zemlya
Much of this island is covered permanently in ice, but low-lying, ice-free areas are tundra. Global warming threatens to unleash nuclear wastes stored in the frozen tundra after the testing of nuclear weapons.

3. Yamal Peninsula
Developers have quickly moved into this region to extract oil. The land is so low-lying that it will sink into the ocean if environmental damage melts the permafrost. Global warming is threatening the traditional way of life of the caribou-herding Nenets people.

4. Yenisey River
This immense river is often frozen from November through May.

5. Dickson
This small port on the Arctic coast is one of the most northerly towns in Russia. The winters are long and dark. The people there depend on fishing, hunting and reindeer farming.

6. Wrangel Island
An island where seals and polar bears breed.

7. Whalebone Alley
On Yttygren Island, this important archaeological site is an ancient monument made by arctic people from the skulls of 60 bowhead whales.

Siberia Facts

▲ In the south-eastern Siberian tundra lies the town of Oimyakon, where a temperature of −70°C (−94°F) was recorded. When it is that cold, your breath freezes and tinkles to the ground with a noise the locals call 'the whispering of the stars'.

▲ The Siberian tundra is so cold that plants grow extremely slowly. Mosses grow about as much in a year as your fingernails grow in a week.

▲ The Siberian tundra belt is about 482 kilometres (300 miles) wide, which is about as far as the distance between St. Louis and Chicago.

POLAR PLANTS

Plants need sunlight and water, as well as soft ground for their roots. But the land near the poles is frozen solid and dark for months on end – and it can be drier than the Sahara. Only the world's toughest plants can survive in this extreme environment.

Imagine what it would be like to live in Greenland. You would need plenty of thick clothes to help keep you warm, including boots and gloves to keep your feet and hands from freezing. In winter, you might want a flashlight for those days when the Sun never seems to rise, and in summer, you would need sunglasses to protect your eyes from the dazzling snow and ice.

People can adapt to life in difficult places, but only if they remember to pack the right equipment. Likewise, but over millions of years, plants can adapt to live in the freezing Arctic and Antarctic, but they have to be pretty remarkable plants to survive.

The biggest threats to a polar plant are the numbing cold, the darkness, the icy winds and the lack of sheltered places in which to

Red bearberry leaves brighten this view of tundra plant life in the Yukon Territory, Canada. Like arctic tundra elsewhere, the Yukon tundra has no trees.

Sun Watchers

Although summer days are long in the tundra, sunlight is weak because the Sun stays low in the sky. To make the most of the weak light, some plants turn around to track the Sun through the sky. The butter-yellow flowers (right) of the arctic poppy look like satellite dishes as they turn to follow the Sun. Just as a satellite dish gathers radio waves and focuses them on an antenna at the centre, so the petals of the arctic poppy focus warmth onto the centre of the flower, helping the seeds grow quickly. Other plants, such as arctic avens, use this trick, too.

grow. But polar plants have overcome all of these problems. Just as you would wrap yourself in a sweater to keep warm, so are the stems and leaves of many arctic plants covered in little furry hairs. Sweaters keep us warm by trapping a layer of air next to our bodies. In the same way, the hairs of arctic plants trap warmer air around them. One arctic plant has such a thick woolly coat that it is named the woolly lousewort.

Plants use sunlight to grow through a process called photosynthesis. They trap the energy in light and use it to combine water and **carbon dioxide** (a gas in the air) to make food. Because the poles are dark throughout winter, plants cannot grow. So they either stay inactive under the ice or die after setting seed, and the seeds wait for the next summer. Tundra plants grow quickly in

the short summer, making good use of the long days to flower and produce seeds as soon as possible before winter begins again. Many tundra plants don't even bother to flower – instead they grow sideways and split into new individuals, making clones of themselves.

Cold and darkness are not the only problems facing polar plants. There are also gales and freezing blizzards that would kill many ordinary plants in minutes. For this reason, most polar plants tend to

Rather than standing tall against the gales, the little arctic dwarf willow grows along the ground. A coat of downy hairs protects it from the cold.

grow very near the ground, where the wind is slower and the temperature slightly warmer. Willows grow as shrubs or trees in warmer parts of the world. In the Arctic, the twisted stems of dwarf willows snake across the ground, growing sideways instead of upwards. Rarely more than several centimetres tall, they escape the worst of the wind and the ice in this way.

Some arctic plants turn the wind to their advantage, using it to help them spread their seeds further and increase their chances of survival. One of the best-known arctic plants, cotton grass, has fluffy heads at the top of its thin stems. The heads produce thousands of very small seeds, which are caught by the wind. They swirl into the air and fly far away to grow in new places.

Despite the cruel conditions, as many as 1,000 species of plants thrive in the arctic region, and 40 different flowering plants grow in Greenland alone. Conditions are different in Antarctica, though, where only two species of flowering plants exist (*see* page 25).

Of the plants that provide food for the creatures of the Arctic, none are more important than those with berries. Although grizzly bears and polar bears are mainly meat-eaters, they are sometimes forced to be vegetarian when prey is in short supply. One of their favourite snacks is the aptly named bearberry. The seeds in bearberries pass through the bear unharmed and sprout if they fall on good ground.

Why No Trees?

One definition of the polar biomes is that they are places where no trees grow. Trees flourish in the taiga biome to the south of the Arctic, but the tundra and polar deserts are treeless. Why? The most obvious answer is that it is too cold. Yet this cannot be the whole explanation, because the spruce trees that grow along the northern edge of the taiga can survive winter temperatures that are even colder than those on the arctic coast.

The main reason that trees do not grow is the permafrost, the permanently frozen ground underneath the surface layers of the thin tundra soil. The permafrost makes it impossible for roots to grow any deeper than several centimetres. Another problem is the lack of shelter from the freezing wind, which stunts growth. And in the polar deserts, there simply isn't enough water for large plants.

In the Polar Garden

Gardeners around the world often divide their plots into different areas, such as rock gardens, rose gardens and wildflower meadows. This may seem an original idea, but it is only a copy of what nature does by itself. In the tundra, for example, plants form different types of gardens depending on how much water is available. In marshy areas, mosses form a layer under other plants, such as grass-like plants called sedges. In less soggy places, small shrubs are common. They burst with berries in summer and turn orange or red

Above: the seed heads of cotton grass are a common sight in the tundra in August. Inuit people use the silky white 'cotton' to stuff pillows and mattresses.

Left: in late summer, bears and other tundra creatures feed on tough black crowberries. People also use these berries to make pies, soups and jellies.

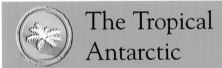

The Tropical Antarctic

The world's coldest continent is one of the best places to find evidence of past eras, because samples are preserved by the cold and undisturbed by human activity. Even a footprint in the moss of Antarctica can last for decades. Paleontologists (scientists who study fossils) have found many remains in Antarctica, including dinosaurs and a huge armadillo the size of a small car.

Such animals could have lived in Antarctica only if it once had more plant life than it does today. Scientists think Antarctica was joined to Africa, India and Australia about 100 million years ago. Together they formed a vast continent – Gondwana – that was north of the equator and had a tropical climate. Fossils of tropical plants remain in Antarctica to this day, hidden under the ice.

in fall. Wildflowers, such as arctic poppies, tend to grow in the rocky parts of the tundra where it is very dry. The rocks themselves may be covered in lichens and mosses – the true survivors of the polar world.

Polar Survivors

Plants do grow in the polar desert of Antarctica, but they are very different from the wildflowers and berries that grow on the tundra. Although life in Antarctica is at its most extreme, algae, lichens and mosses still manage to survive.

By definition, algae are not plants. They are simpler, plant-like organisms that live by photosynthesis, but have no true leaves, stems or roots. In some places, the rocks and ice of Antarctica are turned brilliant red, yellow or green by patches of algae living on the surface.

A lichen is a slightly more sophisticated form of life, made up of a fungus and an alga living together. Lichens are among the hardiest living things on Earth. They can grow on bare rock, and in laboratories they can survive temperatures almost as low as absolute zero (–273°C or –460°F) – the lowest temperature possible. Lichens grow in both Antarctica and the Arctic, colouring

Hidden Life

Two antarctic lakes are thought to contain very different kinds of life. Lake Vanda in the Dry Valleys is permanently frozen over with ice about as thick as the length of a small car. Yet sunlight seeps through, warming the water beneath to a balmy 25°C (77°F) – the temperature of a tropical ocean. In this indoor antarctic swimming pool, a variety of algae, bacteria and other micro-organisms lead a cozy life.

Lake Vostok is about the same size as Lake Ontario but twice as deep. It is also possibly the world's most remarkable lake, because it is buried under about 4 kilometres (2.5 miles) of ice. Because it has been cut off from the rest of the world for millions of years, scientists believe it could contain extraordinary new species or ancient forms of micro-organisms. Scientists are trying to figure out how to explore the lake with robots, in a way that will not contaminate it and kill off any life that may be there.

almost any surface, from rocks to decayed bones, with blotches of orange and gold. They are especially common on darker rocks, which warm up in sunlight more than pale rocks. Lichens provide the starting point for another type of polar survivor: the mosses.

Reindeer moss is not a moss but a type of lichen, eaten by caribou (reindeer). This picture also shows red leaves of a bearberry bush poking through the lichen.

Tundra Plants of North America

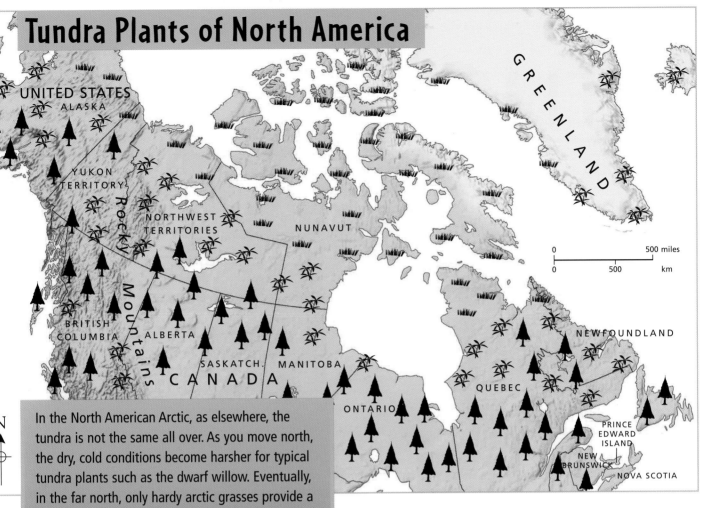

UNITED STATES
ALASKA

GREENLAND

YUKON TERRITORY

NORTHWEST TERRITORIES

NUNAVUT

Rocky Mountains

BRITISH COLUMBIA

ALBERTA

SASKATCH.

MANITOBA

CANADA

ONTARIO

QUEBEC

NEWFOUNDLAND

PRINCE EDWARD ISLAND

NEW BRUNSWICK

NOVA SCOTIA

0   500 miles
0   500   km

N

In the North American Arctic, as elsewhere, the tundra is not the same all over. As you move north, the dry, cold conditions become harsher for typical tundra plants such as the dwarf willow. Eventually, in the far north, only hardy arctic grasses provide a sparse cover on the ground. In the south, the tundra plants are mixed with the conifer forests of the taiga for many miles. Tundra plants also live much further south on the high ground of the Rockies.

Conifer trees form the forests of the taiga.

Dwarf willow is a shrub that can grow in tundra but not in polar desert.

Hardy arctic grasses sparsely cover the ground in dry tundra and polar desert.

By coating rocks with a rough surface, lichens give mosses a foothold in which to grow. Crevices in the moss and lichen trap wind-blown dirt, forming a thin layer of soil. This soil provides anchorage and nutrients for Antarctica's only two flowering plant species: antarctic hairgrass and pearlwort. Both live only in the Antarctic Peninsula, where the climate is milder than in the continent's interior.

Below: mainland Antarctica's only flowering plants, antarctic hairgrass (upper plant) and pearlwort (lower plant) shelter in a moss-lined rock crevice.

ICELAND

Iceland is a striking mixture of hot and cold, famous for huge glaciers, active volcanoes and geysers. A warm ocean current makes the island warmer than most Arctic lands, but the plant life is mainly tundra.

The Vatna Glacier is an ice cap covering the highlands of southern Iceland. It gives birth to glaciers that flow to the lowlands, where they melt, forming rivers.

Iceland Facts

▲ Only one mammal, the arctic fox, lived on Iceland before people arrived. People introduced other mammals such as horses, sheep and dogs. Caribou were imported from Norway in the 18th century and raised as livestock. Rats, mice and mink were carried to the island accidentally on ships.

▲ There are more than 200 volcanoes on Iceland, many of them still active.

▲ Vatna Glacier is as large in area as all the other glaciers of Europe combined.

▲ All the world's geysers are named after a spring called Great Geysir in Iceland. It shoots a jet of hot water 60 metres (200 feet) high into the air.

1. Reykjavik
The capital of Iceland.

2. Westfjords
This mountainous region is a stronghold of Iceland's largest bird, the rare white-tailed eagle, also called the grey sea eagle.

3. Great Geysir
The country's most spectacular geyser.

4. Mount Hekla
A large volcano that has erupted many times, most recently in 1970. In the past, ash from Iceland's volcanoes has caused acid rain to fall in other countries, including Scotland.

5. Desert
Since people settled in Iceland in the year 875, farm animals have overgrazed the fragile tundra plant life. Now, one-third of Iceland is barren desert, even though Iceland's climate is moist.

6. Mount Hvannadals
At 2,119 metres (6,952 feet), this is Iceland's highest mountain.

7. Lake Myvatn
Teeming with ducks and other birdlife, one of the natural wonders of the world.

8. Vatna Glacier
A huge glacier in southeast Iceland. Global warming has sped its flow into the ocean.

 The World's Biggest Duck Pond

It is easy to see why Lake Myvatn is one of Iceland's biggest tourist attractions. Not only is it stunningly beautiful, it is also home to more species of ducks (15 in all) than any other lake in the world. Around the lake are volcanic craters, bubbling mud pools, hot springs and other signs of volcanic activity. Algae flourish in the lake's mineral-rich water, providing food for crabs and midges, and these in turn feed fish and birds. Lake Myvatn means 'Lake Midge'. Although the swarms of midges are unpopular with the tourists, they are one of the reasons why wildlife flourishes there.

POLAR ANIMALS

Did you know that the hair on a polar bear can carry sunlight, like tiny fibre-optic cables? Or that seagulls keep their legs much colder than their body to avoid losing heat? These are just two of the ingenious ways in which animals survive the hardships of life at the poles.

The different climates of the arctic and antarctic regions mean very different types of plants grow in each place. Likewise, the animals living near the north and south poles are also different. In the arctic tundra there are lots of land **mammals**, including grizzly bears, foxes, caribou, musk oxen and lemmings. In Antarctica, however, there are no native land mammals. Nearly all the animals of Antarctica live near the ocean and must return there to survive the winter or find food. The only animals that live permanently on land are tiny insects and mites.

Polar Ecosystems

Just like in any other biome, the organisms of the polar biomes depend on each other to survive. The community of plants, animals and other organisms, together with their physical environment, make up what we call an **ecosystem**. Nearly all Earth's ecosystems are maintained by energy from the Sun. Plants or algae use the Sun's energy to make food, so they can grow and reproduce. **Herbivores** (plant-eating animals) eat the plants, and **carnivores** (flesh-eating animals) eat the herbivores. So the food made by the plants passes along a **food chain**, from plant to herbivore to carnivore.

The ecosystems of the Arctic and Antarctic are unusual. In Antarctica there are very few land plants, so most animals depend on food from the oceans. The base of the food chain is made up of **phytoplankton** – microscopic, plant-like organisms that live on the surface of the ocean. These are eaten by **zooplankton** – tiny organisms that live in the surface water. The zooplankton are eaten by fish, squid, mollusks and other animals, and these provide food for penguins and seals.

Being a warmer and less extreme place than Antarctica, the Arctic is home to many more species. Just as in Antarctica, there is a marine food chain based on phytoplankton. This food chain is very important for animals that come on land to breed, such as seabirds, seals and walruses. But there is also a land-based food chain. At the bottom of the chain are lichens, algae and land plants. At the top are meat-eaters, including wolves, snowy owls, polar bears and people. In between comes everything from bumble bees and wolf spiders to caribou.

 Antarctic Bugs

The largest antarctic animal living permanently on land is a wingless insect relative called a springtail. It grows to 13 millimetres (0.5 inches) long. The continent's biggest native land predator is a mite – a tiny spider-like creature. It weighs less than a ten-thousandth of a gram (0.000004 ounces).

Under Threat

The survival of many polar animals is at risk from human activities. Global warming – due to pollutants in the air – is breaking up and melting ancient ice at unprecedented rates and raising the temperature of the seas. Warmer water prevents nutrients from rising to the water's surface, where microscopic plankton grow. Many fish and crustaceans, such as krill, live off plankton. In turn, these animals are food for whales, seals and birds that migrate hundreds of kilometres to feed and breed in the short polar summer. In this way, the threat to plankton affects all polar animals.

Global warming is breaking up the ice in the Arctic where polar bears hunt for seals. The bears are now forced to travel much further to find enough food. In Antarctica, the breaking up of ice shelves is blocking the migration routes of penguins that come onto the ice to breed.

Global warming and climate change may lead to the extinction of many polar animals. The countries of the world have to reduce their emissions of carbon dioxide and other pollutants that cause global warming to prevent further ecological disaster.

In Antarctica, there are hardly any land plants. Nearly all the animals that live there, such as these chinstrap penguins, live off food from the ocean, such as fish. These penguins are resting on an unusual iceberg made of blue ice.

Life in the Freezer

If you took a monkey from a rainforest and moved it to Antarctica, it would die very quickly. Monkeys are well adapted to the heat and moisture of the tropics, but they cannot survive in a polar desert. All the creatures that live in the polar regions have evolved special characteristics, or adaptations, that help them survive there.

The biggest challenge is staying warm. Many polar animals are **warm-blooded**. Just like people, they keep a constant body temperature, no matter how the temperature of their surroundings varies. Being warm-blooded allows animals to stay active even when their surroundings are freezing cold. In contrast, **cold-blooded** animals, such as lizards and frogs, would become inactive and freeze – so it is not surprising that very few lizards or frogs venture into the Arctic, and none can be found in Antarctica.

Warm-blooded animals need features that stop them from losing heat. Most warm-blooded animals have layers of **insulation** around their body to retain heat. People insulate themselves with clothes, but other

animals, such as polar bears, have a thick fur coat. They also have a layer of fat, or blubber. The blubber acts mainly as an energy store for times when food is hard to find, but it also helps keep in the heat. Seals and walruses also have blubber, but unlike land animals, they have an extra insulating feature. By changing their blood flow, they can keep their blubber layer cool while maintaining a warm temperature deep inside their body. Walruses have so much blubber that they risk overheating when they come onto land.

Arctic wolves, like polar bears, have a thick, layered, insulating coat of fur. The fur holds a layer of warm air around the body and acts as a barrier to cold.

Walruses rest on land a great deal. This way, they spend less energy keeping their body warm in the cold sea. They can use their tusks as picks during fights.

Although they spend much of their time in the ocean, walruses come ashore to rest and breed in large **colonies** on the Arctic coast. To lose heat, they blush – blood flows through the skin, turning their body bright pink.

Walruses use their long whiskers to feel for shellfish on the murky seafloor. With their tusks held out of the way, they grub about for food in the mud, a bit like pigs do. And just as submarines can push their way through sea ice, so a walrus can use its tough head to break ice up to 20 centimetres (8 inches) thick.

Cold Feet

Keeping their feet warm is a particular problem for polar animals. Most of an animal's warmth is in the centre of its body. Any body parts that stick out from the centre, such as legs, arms, ears and a nose, are the first to lose heat in cold weather. To save precious heat energy, some animals have legs that can be colder than the rest of their body. Seagulls and caribou are two examples. Native peoples of the Arctic have long known that the lower parts of a caribou's leg freeze at much lower temperatures than the upper parts. For this reason, they would use the fat – which contains an antifreeze-like substance – from caribou feet to oil the strings of their bows, so that they remain supple and don't freeze.

Big Is Better?

A 19th-century scientist named Carl Bergmann claimed that bigger creatures are better off in cold climates than smaller ones, because they don't lose heat so quickly. Why should this be so? The amount of heat an object can hold depends on its volume (the space it takes up), while the speed it loses heat depends on the area (size) of its surface. Small animals have a higher ratio of surface area to volume, so they lose heat faster. Think how slowly a hot potato cools down, compared to a similar volume of french fries. The fries have more surface area than the potato, so they turn cold much quicker. But size is not the only answer to surviving at the poles. A large animal must find more food to fuel itself than smaller animals, even in winter, when food is hard to find. In addition, small animals can better avoid the cold by staying in burrows.

Sometimes fur and blubber are not enough to beat the cold. The musk oxen of the arctic tundra and the penguins of Antarctica may huddle together to help stay warm. Ptarmigan and small birds fly into fluffy snow banks, or dig themselves into the snow of the tundra with their feet. Cold as this may seem, it is still warmer than standing in a blizzard. Some polar animals have a particular size or shape that helps them cope with the cold. Large, bulky animals generally stand up to the cold better than small animals, for example.

Migrating Mammals

Rather than endure the dark and freezing tundra winter, most caribou migrate south at the end of summer. Every year, more than a million of these arctic deer make a long trek to the forests of the **taiga**, where they find shelter in winter. They return to the tundra on the arctic coastal plains in spring, when

These caribou live in Siberia, which has some of the coldest winters the Arctic has to offer. It is no wonder, then, that the caribou migrate south into the taiga biome, shown here, to find shelter in winter.

they give birth to their calves. Caribou live throughout the tundra and taiga of North America, Europe and Russia, though they are called reindeer in Europe and Russia. The Peary caribou and the Svalbard reindeer live on arctic islands, so they can't move south to escape the winter. They must endure the dark and cold, but when desperate, they attempt dangerous crossings over the sea ice.

Another arctic mammal, the musk ox, does not migrate far, but shifts only a few miles between its summer and winter grazing grounds. In summer, musk oxen eat sedges and willows on low-lying tundra; in winter, they move to ground free of deep snow to eat grasses exposed by the arctic winds. The severe climate is seldom a problem for musk oxen, because their shaggy coats are eight times warmer than sheep's fur and protect them well against harsh blizzards. The most severe blizzards can last for several days, though, and prevent musk oxen from feeding. At such times, they lie down together to deflect the wind. One way musk oxen lower their need for food in winter is to spend little time moving. The less energy they use for movement, the more energy they have to maintain their body temperature.

Hibernating Mammals

The musk ox's method of saving its energy is halfway between staying active for the winter and hibernating completely. To hibernate fully, animals seek shelter, reduce their body temperature, and become inactive, or **dormant**, usually until the winter has passed. During **hibernation**, their heart beats more slowly and they breathe much less often than they do normally. Although they don't eat, their body survives on reserves of stored fat.

Right: on the treeless tundra, there is nowhere for arctic ground squirrels to hide. This one is keeping a lookout for predators while others in its group feed.

Brown bears hibernate in large dens that they construct of snow in the autumn. With its entrance tunnel, small living room and air hole, a bear's den can be a cozy place to spend the winter. The snow keeps out the cold, and the bear's body heat (and that of its cubs) keeps the den warm. A bear also prepares for hibernation by building up the fat on its body. The fat provides water as well as food for the long winter months.

Grizzly bears are the best-known type of brown bear. They have grey, or 'grizzled', hairs in their fur. But there are several other types of brown bears, including the huge Kodiak bear, which is found in Alaska.

Bears are one of the largest hibernating mammals in the Arctic. Much smaller mammals hibernate, too, including the arctic ground squirrel, which spends two thirds of every year in hibernation.

Arctic ground squirrels don't live in trees (there aren't any) but in underground burrows. These provide shelter from **predators** as well as from the cold climate. Lots of animals prey on the ground squirrel – snowy owls hunt them from above, and polar bears try to claw the squirrels out of their holes. The squirrel's hibernation is made up of short periods. During a period, it curls into a ball

South polar skuas are vicious predators. Their favourite food is penguin chicks, but they also eat other seabirds and sometimes even other skuas' chicks.

A flight of snow geese might be a familiar sight as far south as Mexico, but their destination is the arctic tundra, where they raise their chicks in summer.

and allows its body temperature to fall to that of its burrow. If its burrow gets very cold, the squirrel's body might freeze solid, so its brain stays awake and keeps its body temperature above the freezing point. All mammals need sleep, so after two weeks or so, the squirrel warms itself to normal body temperature, relaxes and falls asleep for some hours, before entering its next period of wakeful hibernation.

Migrating Birds

Just as some people fly to warmer places for winter, so birds use their wings to escape the worst of the weather. Most arctic birds spend only their breeding season in the tundra, and fly vast distances south once they have raised their young. Some sandpipers, for example, fly 19,000 kilometres (12,000 miles) south from its arctic nesting grounds, which is like flying from New York to Los Angeles four times. The bird with the most spectacular migration pattern is the arctic tern. It spends the winter

 ## Gone Forever

Casualties of European exploration of the Arctic include Steller's sea cow and the great auk. Steller's sea cow was a sirenian, a relative of dugongs and manatees. It was much larger than its living relatives, growing up to 8 metres (26 feet) long and weighing several tons. It lived in the Bering Sea and was hunted as food and for its oil and skin. It became extinct in 1768. The great auk was a flightless bird that resembled a penguin. It was common on islands off Newfoundland. From the 16th century onward, sailors began to kill the great auk for food, oil and feathers. Numbers of the birds plummeted. In June 1844, collectors clubbed the last two great auks to death for their eggs.

in the ocean around Antarctica. In summer, it flies all the way to its breeding grounds in the arctic tundra.

Almost 50 species of birds thrive south of the antarctic circle, including terns, petrels, fulmars, gulls, shearwaters and albatrosses. In Antarctica, the birds live along the coast because they depend on the sea for food. Most antarctic birds eat shrimp-like animals called krill, fish or squid, but some eat other birds or even seals. Petrels loiter around seabird colonies, hoping to gobble up a penguin chick or feast on a dead seal. But even petrels live in fear of skuas – aggressive

 ## Penguin Points

▲ Penguins live in the Antarctic but not the Arctic.

▲ Penguins can't fly in the air. Rather, they use their wings as flippers for 'flying' underwater.

▲ Fossils found in New Zealand reveal that some prehistoric penguins were as tall as people.

▲ The only penguins to nest on the antarctic mainland are Adélie penguins (below) and emperor penguins. In recent years, the increased rate of break-up of Antarctica's ice has been blocking the ancient migration routes of the penguins.

Early summer in the Russian Arctic is time for red-breasted geese to arrive and begin nesting.

birds that terrorise seabird colonies and readily attack people when threatened.

More birds live in the Arctic than Antarctica. There are several reasons for this: the arctic tundra is nearer to other areas of land; the climate is less harsh; and there are more varied habitats for breeding and feeding. Even so, most birds fly south for the winter and spend just a few months breeding in the Arctic each summer. There are only a few hardy year-round residents, including the ptarmigan, the snowy owl and the raven.

During the breeding season, predators are common in the Arctic, both in the air and on the ground. Airborne predators include eagles and skuas, while land predators include foxes, wolves, bears and ermines (short-tailed arctic weasels).

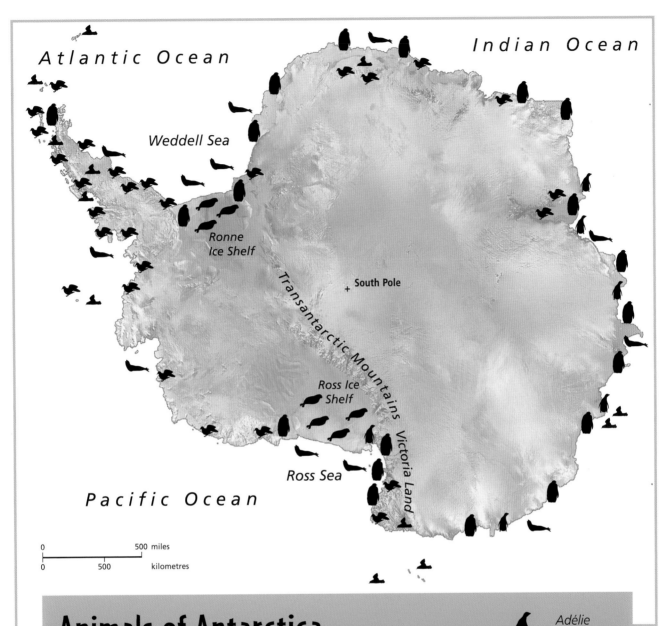

Atlantic Ocean

Indian Ocean

Weddell Sea

Ronne
Ice Shelf

Transantarctic Mountains

+ South Pole

Ross Ice
Shelf

Victoria Land

Ross Sea

Pacific Ocean

| 0 | | 500 | miles |
| 0 | 500 | | kilometres |

Animals of Antarctica

Most of Antarctica is covered with a high dome of ice. Nothing can live on top – it is much too cold and too far from the nearest source of food: the ocean. All antarctic animals live within reach of the ocean. Large colonies of Adélie and emperor penguins roost on rocky coasts and islands around Antarctica. In winter, though, male emperor penguins travel far from the open sea across the ice to incubate their eggs in safety. Predatory birds such as petrels and skuas hunt and scavenge near the coastal penguins, but some fly inland to nest in dry valleys and on outcrops of rock. Ross seals live deep in fields of sea ice, but Weddell seals live even further from the open sea, on the permanently frozen ice shelves. They reach the sea by cutting down through the ice with their teeth.

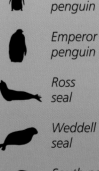

Adélie
penguin

Emperor
penguin

Ross
seal

Weddell
seal

South polar
skua

Snow
petrel

Because there are lots of predators, arctic birds need effective defences. Fulmars vomit on their attackers. Arctic swans trample, bite, batter and hiss at anything that threatens them. And many birds nest together in large colonies, from ducks to guillemots. With so many eyes and ears on the alert in a colony, the risk of being caught unawares by an attacker is much lower.

For migrating birds, timing is everything. They must carefully time their transglobal journeys so they arrive at their breeding grounds at exactly the right time of year. Timing is important in other ways, too. Skuas lay their eggs so the chicks hatch at the same time as those of penguins. This ensures there will be plenty of food around for the hungry young skuas.

Toughest of the Tough

Although some polar creatures shy away from winter by migrating or hibernating, others remain where they are, using a variety of different tricks to survive. Unable to fly away from Antarctica, penguins huddle together to keep warm. The ptarmigan is one of the few arctic birds that doesn't fly south for the winter. It also holds the record for the bird that spends winter closest to the North Pole. When winter approaches, the ptarmigan changes from brown to white and sprouts fluffy feathers on its feet. Its uses its feathered feet to dig tunnels in the snow, where it is much warmer than in the air outside.

Lemmings endure the arctic winter by digging a complicated network of tunnels in the snow. As they dig down to the ground

Dieting Dads

After a female emperor penguin lays her egg, she leaves it to the male to care for and returns to the ocean to feed. Balancing the egg on his feet, the male tucks a flap of bare skin over the egg to keep it warm. He spends more than three months of the bitter Antarctic winter without eating while he looks after the egg. By huddling together (below), the male penguins can limit their heat loss during this time. Even so, they lose half their body weight in these months.

White in Winter

Many polar creatures are white, including polar bears, Dall's sheep, Peary caribou and some gyrfalcons. Others turn white only when the winter comes. These include arctic foxes (left and right), ermines, lemmings, arctic hares and birds such as the ptarmigan. Being white helps animals hide in snow or ice, and so reduces the chance of being spotted by a predator. It also helps predators sneak up on victims without being seen. Some scientists think that white fur is warmer than other colours. White materials reflect heat more than dark materials, so a coat of white fur reflects body heat back towards the skin. The white hairs also contain air spaces that make them even warmer.

surface, they eat whatever plants they find. Similar to hamsters, they have short legs and ears, and lots of brown fur. But in winter they turn white, like many arctic creatures. Lemmings breed very quickly – females give birth to up to nine young at a time, only three weeks after mating. Sometimes the population of lemmings grows so much that many are forced to leave their burrows and migrate elsewhere. The mass migrations happen every few years, when hundreds of lemmings can be seen scampering across the tundra. Occasionally, some fall off cliffs or drown in ponds or the sea by accident, but lemmings do not do this deliberately, as some people think.

Like any other biome, the arctic tundra has scavengers – animals that live off the spoils of others. The arctic fox, for instance, follows polar bears for the remains of their kills. Well-adapted to life in the cold, the fox has a short nose and small ears that reduce

Lemmings survive the arctic winter by gnawing plants, which they find beneath the snow.

heat loss. Its fur is luxurious and even covers the undersides of its feet to keep out the cold. The polar bears it follows are also expert arctic survivors, equally at home on land, on sea ice, or swimming in the chilly ocean. Polar bears prey on seals and young walruses and also scavenge from dead whales. If food is in short supply, they venture inland for berries, grass or whatever they can find. Some polar bears even enter towns to sniff out morsels of food in garbage.

 Polar Warriors

Suppose you had to design an animal to survive life at the North Pole. Could you come up with anything better than a polar bear? A typical polar bear is about 2.1 metres (7 feet) tall and 540 kilograms (1,200 pounds) in weight – as much as five heavyweight wrestlers.

A lot of this weight is fat. Underneath the skin, polar bears have a blanket of blubber several inches deep. It is thickest on the back of the legs and the hind quarters, where the animal is most exposed to the wind. Although blubber is helpful for keeping the bear warm as it plods over the ice, it is even more important when the bear is paddling through the water. Polar bears are excellent

swimmers – they can swim 100 kilometres (60 miles) across open water to reach the ice floes where they hunt. In fact, they are sometimes called sea bears.

Blubber is only one layer of the bear's clothing. Next comes a cosy layer of wool. And on the outside, there is a thick fur coat made up of long, hard guard hairs. Each guard hair works like one of the glass fibres in a fibre-optic cable. Sunlight is carried down the hair to the bear's body, helping warm the skin, which is black. With blubber, wool, and a Sun-heated fur coat, polar bears are so well-insulated that they hardly show up on infrared (heat-sensitive) cameras.

No Way In

Creatures that develop ways of defending themselves against their hunters are more likely to thrive. When musk oxen – which are closer relatives of sheep and goats than cattle – are attacked, they huddle together in a circle, rump-to-rump, protecting their calves between them. That leaves just their heads and their horns exposed, which makes it much easier to defend themselves against predators such as wolves.

Small is Beautiful

Cold conditions may favour large creatures, but the polar regions are also home to many small lifeforms. One of the Arctic's most ferocious little creatures is a shrimp-like animal called an **amphipod**, which lives in the ocean. When a young Inuit fell through the

ice and drowned in the Canadian Arctic some years ago, rescuers were shocked when they found his dead body. Although his clothes were intact, amphipods had picked off and eaten all the flesh from his bones in less than a day.

Lots of insects and spiders live in the arctic tundra. They spend the winter in resting form, usually as eggs, which are not killed by freezing. Once it is warm enough, the insects burst into activity. Mosquitoes hatch from tundra pools and swarm in millions. There are so many mosquitoes that this may be one of the reasons why caribou migrate north to give birth. The insects live both in the taiga, where caribou spend their winters, and in the tundra, where caribou calve. But they appear a whole month later in the tundra. This extra month gives the caribou time to calve and raise their young before the mosquitoes start biting. Other arctic insects include butterflies, crane flies and bumble bees.

Plants and insects must rush to take advantage of the brief arctic summer. This crane fly is soaking up some sunshine on an arctic poppy.

ANTARCTICA

Antarctica is the coldest, driest, windiest, darkest and highest continent on Earth. Nowhere on the planet is less hospitable to life.

Most of Antarctica is covered by ice so thick that only mountaintops show through it.

Fact File

▲ Antarctica has 70 per cent of Earth's freshwater but is one of the driest deserts.

▲ The average temperature of the Antarctic Peninsula increased by 2.5°C (4.5°F) between 1960 and 2010.

▲ On average, Antarctica is three times higher than other continents because of all the ice. The weight of the ice has squashed the land to below sea level in some places.

▲ Antarctica's ice shelves are breaking up. If this continues, it will lead to the extinction of the penguins that breed on the ice.

1. Lambert Glacier
A vast glacier that flows slowly off the mainland and into Amery Ice Shelf.

2. Vostok
This Russian base is officially the coldest place on Earth. The world's lowest ever temperature (−89.2°C or −128.6°F) was recorded there.

3. South Magnetic Pole
The place on Earth's surface that compasses point away from. The magnetic poles slowly change position over time.

4. Dry Valleys
Ice-free, rocky valleys near the Transantarctic Mountains.

5. McMurdo Station
This U.S. base on Ross Island is Antarctica's biggest community, with a summer population of 1,200 and a winter population of 200.

6. Mount Erebus
A gigantic active volcano on Ross Island, at the edge of the Ross Ice Shelf.

7. Transantarctic Mountains
This vast mountain range forms the dividing line between Greater and Lesser Antarctica.

8. South Pole
The most southerly point on Earth.

9. Ross Ice Shelf
A vast shelf of sea ice – about the size of France – that ends in towering cliffs. Massive parts of the shelf have collapsed in recent years.

10. Vinson Massif
Antarctica's tallest mountain, at 5,140 metres (16,864 feet).

11. Antarctic Peninsula
The most northern point of Antarctica. Several of its ice shelves have collapsed in recent years because of warmer ocean currents.

12. Gibbs Point
This rock point on the peninsula was named in 2009 for African-American explorer George W. Gibbs Jr.

The Dry Valleys

It's strange to think that a continent with as much ice as Antarctica could also contain a rocky desert, yet the Dry Valleys have been free of ice for millions of years. They are dry because the nearby mountains hold back glaciers, and because strong winds blow away what little snow falls.

Despite the name, the Dry Valleys contain Antarctica's only river – the Onyx – which flows only in summer and contains beautifully clear water. There are also a few lakes, though these are permanently frozen over.

You might think the Dry Valleys would be devoid of life, but they aren't. They contain moss, microscopic organisms called cyanobacteria, and tiny nematode worms that are just 1 millimetre (0.04 inches) long. However, since 1993 the number of the nematodes appears to have decreased by two-thirds. Scientists are unsure why.

Indian Ocean

Mawson (Australia)

← Amery Ice Shelf

← Lambert Glacier

[1]

[2]

● Vostok (Russia)

+ South Magnetic Pole

[3]

Greater
Antarctica
(East Antarctica)

Dry Valleys **[4]**

[5]

McMurdo (U.S.)

[6]

Mount Erebus

Ross Sea

Transantarctic Mountains

[7]

Ross
Ice Shelf

[8] South Pole +

[9] (!)

Pacific
Ocean

Transantarctic Mountains

Lesser
Antarctica
(West Antarctica)

Ronne
Ice Shelf

Weddell
Sea

Atlantic

Ocean

Vinson Massif

[10]

Antarctic Peninsula

[11] (!)

[12]

South Orkney
Islands

South Shetland Islands

0		500 miles
0	500	kilometres

AUSTRALIA

AFRICA

ANTARCTICA

SOUTH
AMERICA

43

PEOPLE AND THE POLES

Antarctica has always been too cold and desolate for anyone other than scientists and explorers to consider living there, but the Arctic is another matter. People adapted to life in this extreme environment thousands of years ago.

The people who have lived in the Arctic for longest are often called Eskimos. Language experts think the word *eskimo* probably came from the Algonquian language, from a word meaning 'she laces a snowshoe'. Other language experts claim Eskimo means 'eater of raw meat'. Some arctic people do not like being described in this way, because it seems to imply that they lead simple and primitive lives.

Instead, different groups of native peoples living in the Arctic prefer different names. People from the eastern part of the Canadian Arctic are called Inuit, which means 'the people'. One member of the Inuit is called an Inuk. People from the North Slope of Alaska are called Inupiat, while those who live around the Bering Sea prefer to be called Yupik. In Siberia live arctic peoples called Chukchi and Nenet.

The inhabitants of Savissivik in north-western Greenland talk to the rest of the world with the help of this communications dish.

Houses of Ice

In the Inuit language, the word *igloo* simply means 'house'. People often imagine arctic people living in ice igloos – houses made from blocks of ice or snow. But ice igloos are only temporary dwellings used by hunters and travellers in winter – people never spent the entire year in them. Arctic people built more permanent igloos from stones or wood, covered with grass and sometimes lined with animal skins. At fishing and hunting sites, they lived in tents made from animal skins. For bedding, they built a bench out of earth or snow and topped it with heather or moss to make it comfortable. Then they covered it with a rug made from animal skins, which stopped the bed melting and kept the sleeper warm.

The Arctic Life

People have lived in the Arctic lands of Europe, Asia and North America for at least 4,000 years. Inuit, Inupiat and Yupik peoples reached North America by crossing the Bering Strait from Asia. They may have walked across a land bridge that once connected Russia to Alaska, or they may have come by boat. If so, they probably used wooden boats similar to the umiak that they stilll use today. These small boats were traditionally covered with animal hide and often rowed by women of the tribes.

The arctic way of life has changed in many ways, but in the past it consisted largely of hunting and fishing. With so few plants able to survive the extreme climate of the Arctic, meat was the most important source of food. Arctic people studied the changing seasons and the crafty hunting habits of polar bears – the most fearsome land predators. They knew how to catch fish, whales and seals, and how to keep themselves warm. Most of all, they knew how to survive in one of the harshest places on Earth.

Conquering the Poles

In the 16th century, European sailors began exploring the Arctic. They wanted to find a shortcut from the Atlantic to Asia – the Northwest Passage (*see* map). Many of the early explorers are remembered in the names of places around the North Pole. Frobisher Bay and Baffin Island, for example, are named for English sailors Martin Frobisher

Polar Ships

Explorers first sailed to the Arctic in wooden ships. Though sturdy in the open sea, the ships were no match for the treacherous polar ocean. Many ships were crushed like matchsticks as the ice closed in around them. Others crashed into icebergs and were never seen again. Today, steel ships called icebreakers (right) can slice passages through ice, and large submarines are strong enough to break through as they surface. But every captain knows the story of the *Titanic* – the passenger liner that sank in 1912 after hitting an iceberg – and treats the polar oceans with the respect they deserve.

(1535–1594) and William Baffin (1584–1622). In 1616, Baffin sailed further north than anyone had ever gone, and his record lasted more than 200 years. The Davis Strait is named after English sailor John Davis (1550–1605), who explored the seas around Greenland and Labrador. The Bering Strait is named after Danish sailor Vitus Bering

(1680–1741). He was the first European to prove that Alaska and Siberia are not joined.

In 1819, an English explorer named William Parry (1790–1855) sailed almost all the way to the North Magnetic Pole, mapping out a large area of the Arctic as he did so.

Recent satellite images have shown that – because of global warming – it would be possible to now reach the North Pole in an icebreaker in late summer. In 2007, a Russian flag was planted in the seabed 4,200 metres (14,000 feet) underwater at the North Pole. This act caused international friction. As sea routes open up across the Arctic, several countries are likely to complete for regions, where there are rich oil, gas and mineral reserves. Mining will undoubtedly cause pollution and threaten marine life (which is already under threat from global warming).

The North Pole

After exploring the Arctic for many years, U.S. explorer Robert Edwin Peary (1856–1920) made several attempts to reach the North

Polar explorers and scientists must endure air so cold that it freezes the water droplets in their breath.

The Northwest Passage

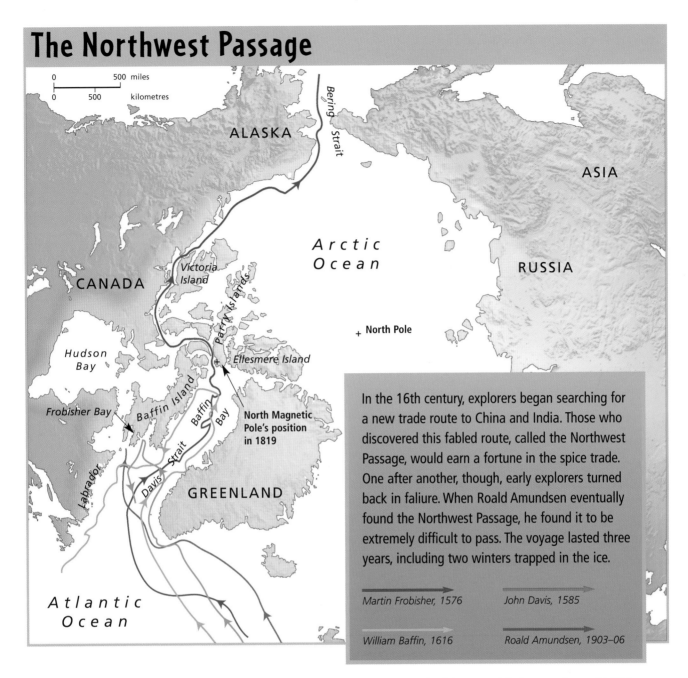

0   500 miles

0   500   kilometres

ALASKA

Bering Strait

ASIA

Arctic
Ocean

RUSSIA

CANADA

Victoria
Island

Parry Islands

+ North Pole

Hudson
Bay

Ellesmere Island

+

Frobisher Bay

Baffin Island

Baffin Bay

North Magnetic
Pole's position
in 1819

Davis Strait

Labrador

GREENLAND

Atlantic
Ocean

In the 16th century, explorers began searching for a new trade route to China and India. Those who discovered this fabled route, called the Northwest Passage, would earn a fortune in the spice trade. One after another, though, early explorers turned back in faliure. When Roald Amundsen eventually found the Northwest Passage, he found it to be extremely difficult to pass. The voyage lasted three years, including two winters trapped in the ice.

Martin Frobisher, 1576   *John Davis, 1585*

William Baffin, 1616   *Roald Amundsen, 1903–06*

Pole. He finally accomplished this amazing feat in 1909, accompanied by African-American explorer Matthew Henson and four Inuit men. There was some doubt about whether Peary had reached the pole first, because another explorer, U.S. doctor Frederick Albert Cook, claimed to have beaten him. Cook's records later proved to be false, and Peary was declared the victor.

It was another two years before anyone reached the South Pole. Two teams of explorers, one from Britain and one from Norway, raced for victory through the harsh conditions of Antarctica. The Norwegian team was led by Roald Amundsen (1872–1928), who had wanted to be the first man to reach the North Pole. When Robert Peary beat him to it, Amundsen decided to head for Antarctica instead. Wisely, he chose to use dogsleds to pull his team's heavy packs, while the British team, led by Robert Scott (1868–1912), hauled their sleds by hand. Amundsen won the race, reaching the South Pole in December 1911. Scott's party arrived one month later, but all five members of the team perished on their way back home. Although Amundsen reached the pole first, both of these courageous men are remembered on the noticeboard that marks the South Pole today. Amundsen later tried to reach the North Pole by sea and by airplane. He died in a plane crash in 1928 trying to rescue another explorer who had vanished at the North Pole.

Modern Arctic People

Since the poles were conquered, people have exploited the Arctic and Antarctica much more, and life for arctic people has changed forever. Once isolated from the rest of the world, their lives today are much more like those of people anywhere.

Transportation has changed a great deal for the Inuit and other arctic peoples. Where

Inuksuit

Arctic people are well-known for their intricate carvings, but they also make huge sculptures by piling up stones or boulders. Each one of these is called an inuksuk, and together they are called inuksuit. Inuksuk means 'looking like a man', and some of these rough stone sculptures do seem to have arms and legs. Sometimes inuksuit were used as signposts or markers in the tundra. An inuksuk might show where the hunting was good, for instance, or it might help arctic people guide herds of caribou. Some people would leave offerings next to them before making hazardous journeys.

they once got around on foot or with dogsleds, today they are more likely to use snowmobiles (motorbikes on skis) or pick-up trucks.

Not everything has changed, though. Arctic people still use the large boats called

Right: between May and August, the Sun never sets at the town of Uummannaq, on the west coast of Greenland.

Above: hunters in the Arctic are more likely to use snowmobiles than dogsleds today. Tents provide temporary homes during hunting trips.

umiak, but today these are more likely to be driven by a gas-powered outboard motor than paddled with oars.

Technology has transformed the way arctic people hunt. Traditionally they threw long harpoons to kill polar bears, seals and other animals. Because the harpoons were made from wood, they floated and were easy to retrieve from the sea. Today, arctic people are just as likely to use a rifle with a telescopic sight. Although many of them try hard to maintain their hunting way of life, many people today buy their food in stores.

We often still think of Inuits and other arctic peoples wearing fur coats and huddling around fires inside their ice igloos. But their home today is a world away from snow houses and animal-skin tents. Although some people still use igloos or tents on hunting trips, many now live in modern, timber-framed houses with central heating. Because their communities are small and remote, arctic people today often use the Internet, both to keep in touch with each other and to make contact with people elsewhere in the world. Many also use citizens' band (CB) radios to pass news to friends and relatives.

What Happened to Arctic Peoples?

People build up resistance to diseases over a long period of time. When two different peoples meet, one may bring diseases to which the other has no defence. This happened when Europeans began to trade regularly with native arctic people. Besides giving them valuable goods, the Europeans gave arctic people smallpox, tuberculosis (TB) and diphtheria. Since arctic people have lower immunity to these diseases, huge numbers died, sometimes leaving whole villages empty. This is one reason why there are fewer native people in the Arctic today.

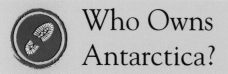

Who Owns Antarctica?

Geologists think that Antarctica may contain huge amounts of oil, gas, coal and other valuable minerals. For this reason, a number of different nations have tried to claim parts of the antarctic continent. However, none of these claims have been recognised by the international community.

Instead, 12 nations signed an agreement called the Antarctic Treaty, which says that no one can develop Antarctica. The treaty came into force in 1961 and bans oil and mineral exploration indefinitely. By 2008, there were 46 signatories.

All these nations agree that Antarctica should be used for peaceful scientific research only. But this does not mean Antarctica is completely protected. The countries that signed the treaty could agree to rewrite it at any time.

Arctic Culture

The Inuit and other arctic peoples were good at making the best of the things that surrounded them. They knew how to transform caribou into clothes or boots, and how to make bedding from the hair of musk oxen. They turned bird skins inside out to make slippers, and put fur on the soles of their boots to walk silently when hunting. Polar bears have fur on the soles of their feet for the same reason. Today, of course, many arctic people prefer to wear anoraks (which is an Inuit word) and boots made in factories.

Arctic life has changed in many ways, through contact with other peoples and with the arrival of modern technology. Some of the changes have made life easier for arctic people. Others, such as diseases carried by European sailors, have threatened their very existence.

Although early Arctic explorers believed the native arctic tribes were simple people, they were advanced in many ways. The first native settlers arrived in North America with pottery, lamps, needles and sophisticated ivory tools. Archaeologists (people who study past civilisations) have found remains of these items in the places where

The Chukchi people live in east Siberia, across the Bering Sea from Alaska. Some were caribou herders while others hunted sea mammals. This Chukchi girl is dancing around her animal-skin tent, called a yarang.

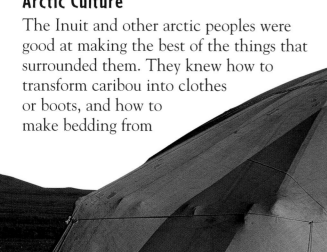

THE UNITED STATES OF AMERICA
WELCOMES YOU TO
AMUNDSEN – SCOTT SOUTH POLE STATION

arctic people once lived. The ancient arctic peoples' tools and their knowledge of animals and plants were very important in allowing them to thrive in the Arctic.

Arctic peoples have always had a lively culture. Much of it is based on their life as a hunting people. Their harpoons were often highly decorated with intricate patterns. Since ancient times, they have carved little figures of the animals they hunted from ivory, soapstone and wood.

Arctic people do not hunt all the time – they also like to relax and enjoy themselves. Singing and dancing are very important in their communities, and huge feasts are regular events. In Alaska, hunters hold a joyous celebration at the end of every whaling season. The person who catches the most whale meat is flung up and down on a trampoline made out of walrus hide stretched over whale ribs.

Antarctic Science

Many people live in the Arctic, but much fewer live inside the antarctic circle. Thousands of tourists visit Antarctica each year by ship. Although many people are concerned of that these visitors and their boats are a threat to the environment, contaminating its pristine wilderness. Apart from tourists, about 4,000 scientists live in some 60 research bases around the continent, including U.S. one at the South Pole (above).

Today, many scientists in Antarctica investigate the atmosphere and the ice. They are monitoring and trying to understand ways of tackling two of Earth's biggest impending problems: global warming and the hole in the ozone layer. Other scientists in Antarctica include climatologists trying to understand the weather of this unusual place and how it affects the rest of the planet. Zoologists and microbiologists examine antarctic life; geologists look at meteorites and the movement of Earth's crust; and astronomers study the Sun and Universe. Not all the scientists who study Antarctica are based there. Some research the continent from laboratories in places such as Great Britain and the United States. Polar animals tagged with radio transmitters can be tracked by satellite and studied from anywhere.

GREENLAND

Greenland contains very little in the way of green land. Three quarters of the country lies inside the arctic circle, and most of it is a polar desert, covered in ice. The few people who live in Greenland inhabit the tundra regions around the coast of the country.

Greenland Facts

▲ The ice on Greenland is, on average, almost 1.6 kilometres (1 mile) thick. The weight of all the ice has made the land underneath sag below sea level. However, global warming is significantly reducing Greenland's ice mass.

▲ Greenland was given its name by Eric the Red, a Norwegian explorer. He thought that if he made the country sound like a nice place, people would want to move there from Iceland.

▲ Greenland's official name is Kalaallit Nunaat, which means 'Greenlander's Country'. It is a self-governing country within the Kingdom of Denmark.

Icebergs locked in the frozen sea lie in Meteorite Bay in north-western Greenland. The village of Savissivik is icebound for most of the year. A boat brings its supplies once a year, in August.

CANADA
Victoria Island
Nares Strait
Svalbard

① !
Knud Rasmussen Land

Siorapaluk ②
Qaanaaq (Thule)

Northeast Greenland National Park

Greenland Sea

Meteorite Bay → • Savissivik
③ !

Greenland Ice Sheet

Baffin Bay

• Daneborg

GREENLAND

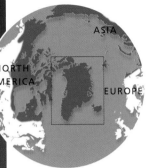

ASIA
NORTH AMERICA
EUROPE

• Uummannaq

⑤

Ilulissat
Jacobshavn Glacier
④
Ittoqqortoormiit (Scoresby Sund)

Disko Bay
Sisimiut
⑥
Kangerlussuaq
⑦
Gunnbjørn ▲

Denmark Strait
Arctic circle

Tasiilak (Ammassalik) • • Kulusuk

ICELAND

Nuuk (Godthåb) ⑧

N

Atlantic Ocean

0   500 miles
0   500   km

Qaqortok • *Paradisdalen*
Nanortalik • ⑨ !

1. Nares Strait
A narrow sea passage between Greenland and Ellesmere Island. Global warming is making the passage more navigable.

2. Siorapaluk
Only 1,362 kilometres (846 miles) from the North Pole, this is the most northern village on Earth.

3. Greenland Ice Sheet
This is the world's second-largest ice sheet, after Antarctica's. It covers 85 per cent of the land in Greenland, but is melting at an unprecedented rate because of global warming.

4. Jakobshavn Glacier
The Jakobshavn Glacier flows up to 30 metres (100 feet) a day as it moves away from the Greenland Ice Sheet, making it one of the world's fastest glaciers.

5. Ittoqqortoormiit
This small town borders the world's largest national park.

6. Sisimiut
Greenland's second-largest town contains the country's only outdoor swimming pool.

7. Kangerlussuaq
A long fjord where the country's main airport is located.

8. Nuuk
The capital of Greenland (also known as Godthåb).

9. Paradisdalen
An important nature reserve containing the only woodland in Greenland. Scientists monitor ozone depletion here.

The World's Biggest National Park

The enormous Greenland National Park is the largest protected area for wildlife in the world. With numerous different habitats, including tundra, fjords, glaciers, lakes and rivers, the park is home to many different animals and birds. The animal residents include polar bears, caribou, walruses, musk oxen and wolves. Among the birds are the snowy owl and the gyrfalcon, a grey-white bird of prey found in much of the Arctic.

No people are allowed to live in the park, but native people from the town of Ittoqqortoormiit are still permitted to hunt there. Because there are no roads, visitors get around by dogsled.

THE FUTURE

The poles were once remote enough to escape the influence of the modern world. Now, climate change, industry and pollution are all changing the polar biomes forever.

People once believed that Earth was a vast place of wild beauty. No matter what they did to it or how much they took out of it, the planet would always heal itself and recover. Today, few places remain untouched by human activities, and Earth seems a much smaller planet than it used to. From coral reefs to tropical forests, many habitats are under threat of destruction. The polar regions, which are among the most remote places on Earth, are changing drastically and most likely permanently. No one knows what the future holds for the Arctic and Antarctica, or whether these ice-covered worlds will even exist in the coming centuries.

The Warming World

Earth's climate warms up and cools down naturally over the centuries. In the past, there have been many **ice ages**, when huge parts of the sea froze over, and many interglacials (periods between the ice ages), when everything warmed up again. Today, Earth's climate is changing for a different reason. Most scientists now believe Earth is

heating up because of carbon dioxide and other gases released into the atmosphere by people.

Carbon dioxide forms when we burn fossil fuels, such as gasoline or coal. The gas acts like the glass in a greenhouse, trapping heat inside Earth's **atmosphere** and gradually making the temperature rise. Although global warming is changing the whole

Melting glaciers crash into the sea at Kenai Fjords National Park, Alaska. Such glaciers will disappear altogether if Earth's climate gets much warmer.

Climate Change

Global warming as a result of carbon dioxide emissions – such as from factories – means that the world as a whole becomes warmer. In places such as New York or Los Angeles, that does not only mean that the days are warmer. The weather becomes more intense and unpredictable – there are likely to be more heatwaves, floods and droughts. But for the polar regions, global warming is disastrous. As the world warms up, the ice on Antarctica and Greenland is melting. Meltwater running into the sea is slowly raising sea levels, causing low-lying coastal areas to disappear underwater. Ice in the Arctic Ocean is also melting, but it won't affect sea levels as much because the ice is already in the water.

of the planet, it is especially damaging to the polar regions and the plants, animals and people who live there.

Scientists know that global warming is already be having an impact on life at the poles. There is much less sea ice around Antarctica than there used to be, and huge numbers of penguins have disappeared. In the eastern Canadian Arctic, caribou numbers have fallen drastically because there is more snow than there used to be. Elsewhere in the Arctic, however, caribou numbers have risen, perhaps because warmer summers have made their food more abundant.

Plants and animals in warmer parts of the world might be able to survive global warming by moving to cooler places as the world warms up. But the species at the poles simply have nowhere else to go.

The Ozone Holes

The Sun gives life to almost everything on Earth, but sunlight also contains **ultraviolet** light, which is harmful to plants, animals and people. Normally, an outer part of Earth's atmosphere called the ozone layer screens out some of this dangerous light. The ozone

 Climate Change

Global warming is raising sea levels by melting polar ice. The huge ice sheet that covers Lesser Antarctica is collapsing. If all of it crumbles into the ocean, sea levels will rise by at least 5 metres (17 feet) worldwide, and low-lying cities, like Miami and New Orleans, would disappear underwater (right). If all of Greenland's ice sheet melts, sea levels will go up 6 metres (20 feet). And if the colossal Greater Antarctica ice sheet melted, sea levels would go up another 61 metres (200 feet). Scientists are continually revising their estimates of when the ice caps will melt if global warming continues. Some predict it may be decades away, others much sooner.

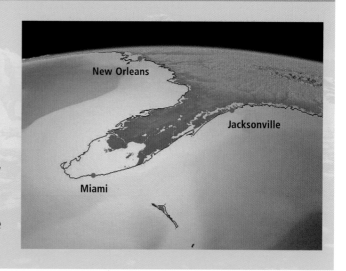

Antarctic scientists use helium-filled weather balloons to study the ozone hole high over Antarctica. These researchers have adapted a balloon to photograph penguin colonies.

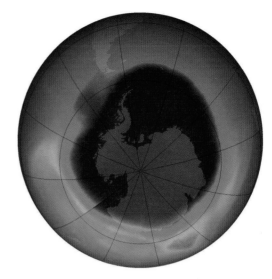

The deep blue area in this satellite picture is the ozone hole over the continent of Antarctica in 2009. There is also a smaller ozone hole over the Arctic.

 ## Disaster in Alaska

The environment paid a high price for arctic oil in 1989, when an oil tanker, the *Exxon Valdez*, ran into a rocky reef in Prince William Sound, Alaska, and its contents leaked into the sea. It wasn't the world's biggest oil spill, but it was one of the most dramatic - thousands of fish, seabirds and otters perished in the resulting slick. The accident proved very expensive for the Exxon oil company. It had to pay about £635 million to clean up the area, and the local fishermen sued the company for £3 billion for the economic damage it caused them. More than 20 years on, many Alaskan beaches still have a layer of oil from the spill trapped just beneath their gravelly surface layers.

works like a thin layer of sunblock spread over the whole Earth. But chemicals released into the atmosphere from such inventions as the aerosol can and refrigerator have eaten away at the ozone layer, and much more ultraviolet light can now get through.

Scientists found the first hole in the ozone layer over Antarctica in 1985, and another hole was discovered over the Arctic about a decade later. Almost every year since then, the ozone holes have grown in size. In 2006, the hole over Antarctica was 27.5 million square kilometres (10.6 million square miles) – about three times the area of the United States.

Without the ozone layer, living things are much more at risk from ultraviolet radiation.

Off-road vehicles crush the slow-growing plants of the tundra, leaving scars that can take decades to heal.

For people, this means more chance of skin cancer and cataracts (a clouding of the eyes that can lead to blindness). Ultraviolet radiation slows down the growth of phytoplankton in the ocean and can even stop them growing altogether. It also damages the DNA of many animals, which can harm the way they grow and reproduce.

An international treaty – the Montreal Protocol – was established in 1989 to globally phase out the chemicals causing ozone depletion. The levels of these chemicals are now on the decrease in the atmosphere, and some scientists predict that the ozone layer may recover by 2050.

Oil and Gas

People have long seen the poles as a source of great wealth. In the 18th and 19th centuries, millions of furs were exported from the Arctic by ship to Britain and North America. More recently, Alaska and Siberia have produced vast amounts of oil and natural gas. This has meant the construction of oil rigs, oil-handling complexes, and some of the biggest pipelines on Earth. The gleaming Trans-Alaska pipeline, for example, runs all

the way from Prudhoe Bay on the north coast of Alaska to Valdez on the south coast. The oil industry has also brought new highways and towns to what used to be wilderness.

Many people see such changes as progress. The world needs oil, and it must come from somewhere. Oil has brought wealth to people of the Arctic, helping them build homes and schools. But not all agree that a growing oil industry is a sign of progress. Highways, towns and factories can damage the arctic wilderness, and oil slicks like the one from the *Exxon Valdez* tanker in 1989 are a constant threat. As the world's need for oil increases, pressure

 ## Oil Versus Wildlife

Whether or not to drill for oil and gas in Alaska's Arctic National Wildlife Refuge (below) has been a political controversy in the United States since the 1970s. Most of the refuge is classified as protected wilderness, but the coastal plain in the north never had full wilderness status. Fuel prices in the United States rose in 2007–2008 and plans were made to explore the coastal plain. If Congress approves this, new oil-drilling plants will appear on the northern coast, taking the place of important breeding sites for polar bears and caribou. The refuge has many supporters, including President Barack Obama, which offers hope that this wilderness will remain pristine.

grows to build oil wells in more remote places, including now-accessible areas of the Arctic Ocean. Today, environmentalists are worried by plans to drill and extract oil from the Arctic National Wildlife Refuge in north-east Alaska. Although the world's nations have agreed not to take oil out of Antarctica, there may come a time when they change their minds. No one knows what effect that would have on the world's last, untouched areas of wilderness.

Saving the Planet

With huge threats like global warming and the ozone hole, the future looks uncertain for the wildlife of the arctic tundra and polar deserts. But things may not be as bad as they seem. Animals such as Steller's sea cow became extinct in the Arctic because people once paid too little attention to the effect we have on the planet. World leaders now recognise climate change as a result of global warming and are taking steps to reduce their nations' emissions of carbon dioxide and ban the chemicals that thin the ozone layer. These changes offer hope that the Arctic and Antarctica – and the animals that make them their home – will survive into the future.

Caribou trudge past the Trans-Alaska pipeline. In the late 1980s, the pipeline carried 2 million barrels of oil per day. By 2015, this will fall to half a million barrels. The United States will then have to find new oil reserves, import more oil, or use and develop alternative sources of power.

GLOSSARY

Algonquian a family of Native American languages spoken by people in eastern Canada and the eastern United States

amphibian a cold-blooded animal that spends part of its life in water and part on land, such as a frog, toad or salamander

amphipod a shrimp-like animal. Some amphipods live in the ocean in polar regions.

antarctic circle an imaginary line drawn around the South Pole on which there is midnight Sun for one day in mid-summer

arctic circle an imaginary line drawn around the North Pole on which there is midnight Sun for one day in mid-summer

arid having a dry climate. Deserts are arid.

atmosphere the layer of air around Earth

aurora a colourful glow in the night sky near the poles

biome a major division of the living world, distinguished by its climate and wildlife. Tundra, desert and temperate grasslands are examples of biomes.

blubber a layer of fat under the skin of some water-living mammals such as seals, walruses and whales.

carbon dioxide a gas released when fuel burns. Carbon dioxide is one of the main gases causing global warming.

carnivore a meat-eating animal.

climate the pattern of weather that happens in one place during an average year.

cold-blooded having a body temperature that depends on the surroundings. Reptiles are cold-blooded, for example.

colony a population of animals living in the same place, such as a group of nesting seabirds.

desert a place that receives less than 250 millimetres (10 inches) of rainfall a year

domestic animal an animal kept by people, usually as a pet, farm animal or pack animal.

dormant so inactive as to appear lifeless. Plant seeds often lie dormant until the soil moistens.

ecosystem a collection of living animals and plants that function together with their environment. Ecosystems include food chains.

equator an imaginary line around Earth, midway between the North and South poles.

ermine a type of white weasel that lives on the arctic tundra

evaporate to turn into a gas (vapour). Water becomes part of the air when it evaporates.

fertile able to sustain plant growth. Farmers try to make soil more fertile when growing crops.

food chain scientists can place animals and plants living in one place into a series that links each animal with the plant or animal that it eats. Plants are usually at the bottom of a food chain with large carnivores at the top.

glacier a river of ice that flows slowly off a mountain or ice sheet

global warming the gradual warming of Earth's climate, caused by pollution of the atmosphere

herbivore a plant-eating animal

hibernation a period of dormancy that some animals go through during winter

ice age a period in history when Earth's climate was cooler. The last ice age ended about 10,000 years ago.

iceberg a huge ice block floating in the sea, having broken from a glacier or ice sheet

ice cap a thick layer of ice covering land near the poles. The largest ice cap is on Antarctica.

insulate to keep warm by trapping a layer of still air

ivory a white material that forms the tusks of walruses or elephants

mammal a warm-blooded animal that feeds its young on milk. Mice, bats and whales are all mammals.

ozone a gas that forms a layer in the upper atmosphere. The ozone layer shields Earth from some of the Sun's ultraviolet radiation.

peninsula a narrow strip of land surrounded on three sides by water

permafrost permanently frozen ground under the surface of tundra and polar desert

phytoplankton tiny, plant-like organisms that float in the surface waters of oceans and lakes

polar desert the main biome in Antarctica, the most northern parts of Canada and Greenland. Gets little rain or snow, and the ground is usually barren or covered with snow and ice.

predator an animal that eats other animals

rainforest a lush forest that gets lots of rain. Tropical rainforests grow in the tropics; temperate rainforests grow in cool places, such as the west coast of North America.

shrubland a biome that mainly contains shrubs

species a particular type of organism. Cheetahs are a species, but birds are not, because there are many different types of birds.

taiga a biome in the north of Canada, Europe and Russia that mainly contains conifer trees

temperate between the tropics and the cold, polar regions

temperate forest a biome of the temperate zone that mainly contains broadleaf trees

temperate grassland a biome of the temperate zone that mainly contains grassland

tropical forest forest growing in Earth's tropical zone (near the equator), such as rainforest or monsoon forest

tropical grassland a biome of the tropical zone that mainly contains grassland. Tropical grassland with trees is called savannah.

tundra a biome of the far north, made up of treeless plains covered with small plants

ultraviolet invisible rays from the Sun that are similar to light. Plants use ultraviolet rays to make food.

warm-blooded having a constantly warm body temperature. Mammals and birds are warm-blooded.

water vapour the gas that forms when water evaporates

zooplankton tiny animals and animal-like organisms that live in the surface of oceans and lakes

Further Research

Books

Doherty, C. A. *Arctic People (Native America)*. New York: Chelsea House, 2008.
Lynch, Wayne. *A is for Arctic: Natural Wonders of a Polar World*. Willowdale, Ont., Canada: Firefly Books, 1996.
Silverstein, A., Silverstein, V. B., and L. Silverstein Nunn. *Global Warming (Science Concepts)*. Minneapolis, MN: Twenty-First Century Books, 2009.
Tarbox, A. D. *An Arctic Tundra Food Chain*. Mankato, Mn: Creative Education, 2009.

Websites

Arctic Studies Center: www.mnh.si.edu/arctic
(Information and exhibits about wildlife of the Arctic, its history and its peoples.)
Biomes of the World: www.thewildclassroom.com/biomes/arctictundra.html
(Packed with information about the arctic tundra and other biomes.)
Tundra: edtech.kennesaw.edu/web/tundra.html
(Great research site with a selection of helpful links.)

INDEX

Page numbers in *italics* refer to picture captions.

Alaska 6, 8
  oil exploration 60, 61
  algae 24
alpine tundra 16
Amundsen, Roald 49–50, *49*
Antarctica 7, 42–43, *42*
  animals 17, 28, 29, 37
  Antarctic Circle 12
  climate *10*, *13*, 14, 15
  Dry Valleys 15, *15*, 42
  ownership 52
  in past eras 23
  plants 24–25, *25*
  see also South Pole
Antarctic Treaty 52
Arctic
  Arctic Circle 12
  climate 12–15
  oil and gas 9, 18, 48, 60–61
  people 31, 44–47, 50–53
  see also North Pole
Arctic Ocean 9, 12, 14, 18, 58

Baffin, William 48, *49*
bears 7, *22*, *23*, 34, 39, 40
Bering Strait 9
berries 22, 23, *23*
birds 32, *34*, 35–38, *35*

Canada 7, 8
  arctic people 44
carbon dioxide 21, 29, 57
caribou (reindeer) 4, 31, 32–33, *26*, 28, *32*, 58
climate change 29, 56–58, 61
cyanobacteria 42

Davis, John 48, *49*

Earth, orbit 10
Eskimos see arctic people
explorers 48–50, *48*
Exxon Valdez oil spill 59
extinctions 29, 35

fossils 23
foxes, arctic *26*, 39
Frobisher, Martin 48, *49*

geysers 26
glaciers 26, *57*
global warming 6, 7, 8, 9, 16, 17, 27, 29, 42, 48, 53, 54, 55, 56–58, 61
Gondwana 23
grasses 22, *23*
grassland 5, *5*
great auk 35
Greenland 7, 20, 49, 50, 54–55, *54*
  people 44
grizzly bears 22, 34
ground squirrels *33*, 34

hibernation 33–35
huskies *47*

ice
  melting and break-up 6, 7, 17, 29, 55, 58
Iceland 6, *7*, 26–27
igloos 45, 51
insects 41, *41*

lakes 24
lemmings 38–39, *39*
lichens 24–25, *24*

methane 16
Midnight Sun 12
migration 32–33, 35–36
Montreal Protocol 60
mosses 19, 23, 24–25
musk oxen 32, 33, 41

Myvatn, Lake 27

national parks 55
Native Americans 9
North America, Arctic 8–9, 25
North Pole
  daylight 10, 12
  explorers 49, 50
North Magnetic Pole 9
northern lights *17*
Northwest Passage 48, 49

oil and gas extraction 9, 18, 48, 60–61
oil spills 59
ozone holes 53, 58–60, *59*

Parry, William 48
Peary, Robert Edwin 48–49
penguins 29, *29*, 36, 38, 42, 58
permafrost 15, 16, 18, 22
polar bears 29, 40
pollution 16, 29, 48

rainfall *12*, 14, 15
reindeer see caribou
reindeer moss *24*
rocks, wind-sculpted *13*
science 53, 59

Scott, Robert 49–50
sea levels 58
seasons 12, 16–17
ships 48
Siberia 7, 18–19
  animals *32*
  arctic people 44, *47*, 52
  tundra 7, 18–19
  soil 15, 16, 18, 22
South Pole
  climate 15
  daylight 12
  explorers 49–50
  U.S. base at 53
springtails 28
Steller's sea cow 35, *35*

taiga 4, 22, 25, 32–33, 41
temperature 13, 14, *14*, 15, 19
threatened species 29
tourism 53

Vanda, Lake 24
ventifacts *13*
volcanoes 6, 26
Vostok, Lake 24

walruses 30–31, *31*
willows, dwarf *21*, 22
wolves, arctic 30

Picture Credits